500 FACTS
Predators

500 FACTS
Predators

Miles Kelly

First published in 2010 by Miles Kelly Publishing Ltd
Harding's Barn, Bardfield End Green, Thaxted, Essex, CM6 3PX, UK

Copyright © Miles Kelly Publishing Ltd 2010

2 4 6 8 10 9 7 5 3 1

Editorial Director Belinda Gallagher
Art Director Jo Brewer
Cover Designer Simon Lee
Designers Candice Bekir, Joe Jones,
Louisa Leitao, Alix Wood, Andrea Slane
Junior Designer Kayleigh Allen
Editors Rosie McGuire, Sarah Parkin, Claire Philip
Indexer Indexing Specialists (UK) Ltd
Production Manager Elizabeth Collins
Reprographics Anthony Cambray, Stephan Davis, Jennifer Hunt, Ian Paulyn
Assets Manager Bethan Ellish
Contributors Camilla de la Bedoyere, Steve Parker, Barbara Taylor

ISBN 978-1-84810-312-2

Printed in China

British Library Cataloguing-in-Publication Data
A catalogue record for this book is available from the British Library

Made with paper from a sustainable forest

Contents

Cats – cute or killers?

1 **All cats, big and small, are killers.** Their bodies are perfectly designed to find, chase and kill animals. Unlike other hunters, such as dogs and bears, cats only eat meat. They are the supreme predators of the animal world and are amongst the most intelligent, beautiful, graceful and athletic of all creatures on our planet. While small cats have found a place in our hearts and our homes, big cats are trying to survive in a world that is taking away the space and freedom they need.

▼ The agile caracal lives in Africa and the Middle East. It hunts rats, hares, birds and baby mammals such as antelope and wild pigs.

Big, bigger, biggest!

2 **All members of the cat family are mammals.** They are all strong but swift and most can climb trees easily. Their faces are rounded and their muzzles short. Cats are predators, which means that they hunt other animals and their teeth are suitable for catching, killing and eating their prey. All cats have excellent eyesight.

▲ The Siberian tiger is covered with thick fur that keeps it warm during the winter months.

3 **The tiger is not only the biggest cat, it is also one of the largest carnivores, or meat eaters, living on land.** Of all tigers, Siberian tigers are the biggest. They may weigh as much as 350 kilograms and can measure 3 metres in length.

MAKE A MONSTER CAT

You will need:
2 cups plain flour   1 cup salt
1 cup water   varnish or paint
  bowl spoon   baking tray
1. Put the flour into a bowl.
   Add the salt and water.
2. Mix to form a smooth dough
   and mould into a cat shape.
3. Put your models onto a greased
   baking tray. Bake at gas mark
   1 or 120°C for one to three
   hours. Once cool, paint or
   varnish your model.

▲ A jaguar's spots look like rosettes and often have a dark smudge in the centre.

6 The nimble cheetah does not need to be big in order to succeed. It has developed into one of the world's greatest predators, proving that skill and speed can make up for a lack of bulky muscles.

7 Sabre-toothed cats became extinct about 10,000 years ago. *Smilodon* was the most famous sabre-toothed cat. It was the size of a large lion and its canine teeth were a massive 25 centimetres long!

4 Jaguars are the biggest cats in the Americas. They measure up to 2.7 metres in length and can weigh an impressive 158 kilograms, which makes them the third largest big cat.

5 Lions hunt in groups called prides. This means that they can catch much larger animals than other big cats that hunt alone. By living and hunting together all the lions in the group eat regularly. Male lions usually eat first, even though the females do most of the hunting.

▲ *Smilodon* probably stabbed thick-skinned animals with its huge teeth.

Where in the world?

8 **Big cats are found mainly in Africa, Eurasia and the Americas.** Where an animal lives is called its habitat. Big cats have adapted to live in a wide range of habitats, from sun-baked deserts to the snow-covered forests of Siberia. Most big cats live in hot countries where there are plenty of animals for them to hunt.

▼ There are about 37 species, or types, of cat found in the world today. Most cats are solitary forest-dwellers.

North America

South America

▶ North, Central and South America are known as the New World. Jaguars, ocelots, margays and pumas, such as the one shown here, are all found in this area.

9 **Jaguars and pumas are cats of the Americas, or New World.** While some jaguars are found in Central America, they have the best chance of surviving in the Amazon basin of Brazil. Here, the thick rainforest offers them protection from hunters. Pumas can live further north and south than any other species of large land mammal on Earth. They are found from the southernmost tip of Argentina, all the way north to Canada.

▲ The jaguar is best adapted to wetland habitats such as swamps and flooded forests.

◀ Tigers are only found in small regions of southern and eastern Asia. They live in a range of habitats, from tropical forests to Siberian woodlands.

10 The mighty tiger once roamed from south and Southeast Asia, all the way to the Russian Far East. Now it only survives in little pockets of land in these areas. Tigers have lost their habitat to humans who want to farm and live on the land that was once ruled by these huge animals.

Europe   Asia

Africa

Oceania

▲ Cheetahs live in Africa and western Asia. Their habitat is open grasslands.

11 Millions of years ago the Americas were joined to Europe, Africa and Asia. The ancestors of modern cats were able to move across this huge landmass. But Australia, New Zealand and New Guinea separated from the other continents before cats appeared. That is why no cats are native to these places.

▲ Lions live in Africa. A small number, called Asiatic lions, survive in the Gir Forest of southern Asia.

12 Africa is home to many big cats including cheetahs, lions and leopards. Lions live on vast grasslands called the savannah. Their pale fur is the perfect colour to blend in with the dried grasses of the open plains. Cheetahs also hunt on the savannah, but tend to do so during the day, when the other big cats are resting.

King of the jungle

▶ Lions are often incorrectly referred to as 'kings of the jungle'. However, it is tigers, not lions, that are at home in this environment. Tigers are endangered, which means that if we do not do enough to save them, they may soon become extinct.

13 **The tiger is the largest of all the cats and also one of the hardest to find.** Tigers live deep in the jungle where huge trees block out the sunlight, helping them to blend into the murky darkness. Their stripes camouflage them as they tread silently through the dappled shadows. This coat is also perfect for hiding the tiger in long grass.

14 **Tigers hunt by stealth.** They hunt at night, when they can creep up on their prey. Tigers may travel several kilometres each night, roaming along tracks, searching for their victims. Tigers hunt for deer, wild pigs, cattle, monkeys and reptiles. They will even kill young elephants or rhinoceroses.

15 **Tigers love swimming.** When it is hot they may take a dip in lakes and rivers to cool down. They are good swimmers and can make their way across large stretches of water.

16 Although they are powerful hunters, tigers may have to stalk 20 animals before they manage to catch just one. They normally kill once every five to six days and eat up to 40 kilograms of meat in one go! Tigers often return to a kill for several days until they have finished it, or scavengers have carried it away.

QUIZ
1. Why do tigers have stripes?
2. What name is given to animals that eat food that's been left by others?
3. If you were walking in a tiger's forest, how could you try to keep yourself safe?

Answers:
1. A stripy coat helps to camouflage them in the forest. 2. Scavengers, e.g. hyenas and vultures. 3. You could wear a mask on the back of your head

▼ People who need to go into the tigers' forest in Sundarban in east India and Bangladesh, wear masks on the back of their heads. This confuses the tigers into leaving them alone.

18 No two tigers have the same pattern on their coats. White tigers with black stripes are occasionally seen in the wild and are bred in zoos because they are very popular with visitors. Although they don't look like their parents, these tigers are not different in any other way.

▶ White tigers are rare in the wild. This white tiger cub is less likely to survive because its coat does not provide good camouflage.

17 Bengal tigers have a reputation as 'man-eaters'. Tigers don't usually eat people unless they are too sick or old to find other prey, but some tigers prefer the taste of human flesh. Between 1956 and 1983, more than 1500 people were killed by tigers in one region alone.

Jaws and claws

19 **Animals have teeth that are best suited to the types of food they eat.** Cats have long, sharp front teeth to bite and kill their prey. They also have strong back teeth to tear and chew pieces of meat.

20 **Catching, killing and eating other animals is a tough job.** In order to be successful hunters, cats need to have special teeth. Their pointy teeth are called canines. These are especially good for killing or holding onto prey. Behind the canines are carnassials. These teeth are ultra-sharp and they work like a pair of scissors to slice up flesh.

▼ This leopard has killed a gazelle. Leopards drag their prey up into trees where it is out of the reach of other hungry predators and scavengers.

21 Cat tongues are very rough! The scratchy surface is ideal for scraping meat off bones. Cats can make their tongues into a scoop shape, which means that they can take big gulps of water when they are thirsty.

▶ Each claw on this lion's paw is curved and very sharp – a perfect tool for digging into its prey.

Pad

Claw

◀ A cat's tongue feels rough because it is covered in hard spikes, or papillae.

22 The paws of big cats and pet cats are very similar. All cats have paws that are armed with sharp, deadly daggers – claws. The bottom surface of each paw has soft pads that are surrounded by tufty fur to muffle the sound of every footstep.

True or false?

1. Cats can make their tongues into a scoop shape.
2. Cats have five claws on their back paws.
3. The spikes on a cat's tongue are called papillae.

Answers:
1. True 2. False – they have four 3. True

Going solo

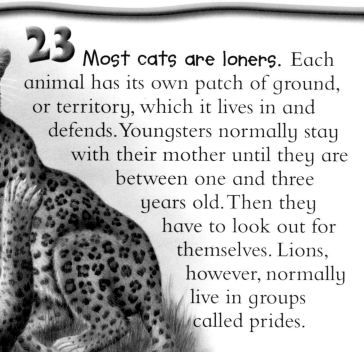

23 **Most cats are loners.** Each animal has its own patch of ground, or territory, which it lives in and defends. Youngsters normally stay with their mother until they are between one and three years old. Then they have to look out for themselves. Lions, however, normally live in groups called prides.

◀ A fight between two leopards over a territory can be extremely fierce and can even be a fight to the death.

I DON'T BELIEVE IT!
Young male lions get thrown out of the pride at about three years old, and spend their 'teenage' years roaming the plains, alone or with their brothers and cousins.

24 **Lions live together.** No one knows why lions live in groups. It may have something to do with their habitat. Hunting on the open grasslands might be easier in a group. Also, it's hard to hide your supper from scavengers, such as hyenas and vultures, when there are few bushes and trees. Maybe a group of lions can send a pack of nosy hyenas on their way more easily than a lion could on its own.

25 Cats mark their territory with their scent, which tells other cats to stay away. They do this by spraying urine on trees and bushes around their area. If another cat comes into their territory there may be a fight. Usually, big cats roar at intruders to scare them away rather than fight.

▶ By washing its face, this cheetah cub is putting scent from glands in its chin onto its paws. It can then mark its territory as it walks.

26 Cats' fur also carries a strong scent. Their scent is made by special parts of their body called glands. When cats wash they spread this smell all over their bodies, and as they rub against trees, the smell comes off. This is another way of marking their territory. That is why pet cats rub themselves against your legs – they are making it clear to other cats that you belong to them!

◀ Cats patrol their territories regularly. This jaguar is sniffing a tree to check that its scent is still strong.

Spotted sprinter

27 Cheetahs are the world's fastest land animals and can run as fast as a car. Within two seconds of starting a chase, a cheetah can reach speeds of 75 kilometres an hour, and it soon reaches a top speed of about 105 kilometres an hour. Cheetahs run out of energy after only 30 seconds of sprinting, so if its prey can keep out of the cheetah's jaws for this amount of time, it may escape capture.

28 This big cat lives in the grasslands and deserts of Africa and Middle East and Western Asia. Cheetahs do not often climb trees, as they have difficulty in getting down again. Cubs often hide in bushes so that they can surprise their prey. The word 'cheetah' means 'spotted wind' – the perfect name for this speedy sprinter.

▼ Cheetahs prefer wide open spaces where they can easily spot prey such as gazelles.

29 Like most of the big cats, cheetahs often live alone. Females live in an area called their 'home range', only leaving if food is scarce. When cubs leave their mothers they often stay together in small groups. Eventually the females go off to find their own home ranges, but the cubs may stay together and attack other cheetahs that come too close.

▶ Cheetah mothers keep their cubs hidden until they are old enough to start learning how to hunt.

30 There are usually between four and six cubs in one litter. Sadly, only one cub in every 20 lives to be an adult cheetah. The others are usually killed by lions or hyenas.

31 Cubs have thick tufts of long, white fur on their heads, necks and shoulders. No one knows why they have this hair, but it might make them look bigger and stronger than they really are.

32 Cheetahs kill antelopes by biting their throats, stopping them from getting any air. Cheetahs can spend a whole day eating if they are undisturbed by vultures or lions, which will steal the food if they can.

How fast are these animals?
Put them in order of fastest to slowest:
1. Cheetah 2. Kangaroo
3. Spur-winged goose
4. Thompson's gazelle

Answers: 1 3 4 2

Home on the range

33 Thousands of years ago, nearly half the world's land was covered in grasslands. Since then much of it has been built upon or turned into farmland. This has contributed to the falling numbers of big cats in these areas. Some grasslands are now protected. These places have become sanctuaries for wildlife.

34 Grasslands occur in places where it's too hot for trees, but there is enough rain to stop the land turning into desert. This is called the savannah and it is home to some of the most famous big cats. When it rains, the waterholes fill and the grass grows green. During the dry seasons, the Sun scorches the grass to the colour of sand and big cats struggle to find enough water and food to survive.

35 Grass is the favourite food of animals that graze. Animals such as giraffes, antelope and wildebeest nibble at the grass, or pick leaves off the bushes and trees that litter the plain.

I DON'T BELIEVE IT!
There are now only 12,000 cheetahs left in Africa, and no more than 200 in Western Asia. Many have been killed for their beautiful fur.

◄ Life in open grassland is difficult and dangerous for plant eaters. There are few places to hide from hunters such as cheetahs and lions.

36 Zebra and other grazing animals make a tasty meal for lions and cheetahs. Since there are few trees to hide behind, it is difficult for these big cats to surprise their prey. Cheetahs rely on speed to catch other animals, while lions hunt in a group. These big cats watch a herd of zebra for some time before making their move. They try to spot any creature that is particularly small, weak or old. If they can separate this animal from the rest of the herd, it will be easier to kill.

23

Cub class

37 **Cubs are born helpless and blind.** A group of cubs is called a litter and there are usually between two and four in each one. Cubs depend on their mother's milk for the first few months of life, but gradually their mother will introduce them to titbits of meat that she brings back to the den.

▲ Lion cubs, may stay with their mothers for two years or more before beginning an independent life.

▶ Mother cats such as this puma need to stay alert and on the lookout for danger. Their cubs, or kittens, make an easy target for other predators.

38 **Male lions help to look after their young.** When the lionesses are hunting, the males protect the cubs and play with them. When a hunt is successful the males eat before the females, but often let the cubs eat first. All lions have black tufts of fur on the ends of their tails. The tufts don't seem to have any use except as playthings for lion cubs!

▼ Lion cubs like to play. Even this tortoise is a source of interest. By playing like this, the cubs are learning hunting skills.

39 **The babies of some cats, such as pumas, are called kittens.** Adult pumas are sand-coloured, to provide them with camouflage in the deserts and mountains where they live. Their kittens are born with spots on their fur that gradually fade. Spots are better camouflage for these youngsters, which hide in bushes and undergrowth.

40 **Cubs learn how to hunt from watching their mothers.** Many mother cats teach their babies how to hunt by bringing them small animals that they have captured alive. When they let the animal loose, the cubs or kittens can play with it and practise their hunting skills. It may seem cruel, but it is important that the cubs learn how to look after themselves.

I DON'T BELIEVE IT!

Cubs have a tough time making it to adulthood. Cubs are hidden by their mothers, partly to avoid bumping into any males. Male cats such as tigers kill any cubs that aren't their own.

Sociable simba

41 **Lions are sociable animals.** They live in family groups called prides that normally include between four and six adults, all related, and their cubs. Large prides of perhaps 30 animals develop where there is plenty of food.

► Lionesses give birth to a litter of between one and six cubs. The cubs stay with their mother for over two years.

42 **Unlike other big cats, male and female lions look very different.** They both have sandy-coloured fur that blends into sun-scorched grasslands, but the males have manes of darker hair on their heads and shoulders that make them look powerful and threatening.

43 **The best time to hunt is early morning or evening.** The lionesses prepare an ambush by spreading out and circling their prey. They hunt zebra, wildebeest, impala and buffalo. A group of lionesses has been known to bring down an adult giraffe that was 6 metres tall!

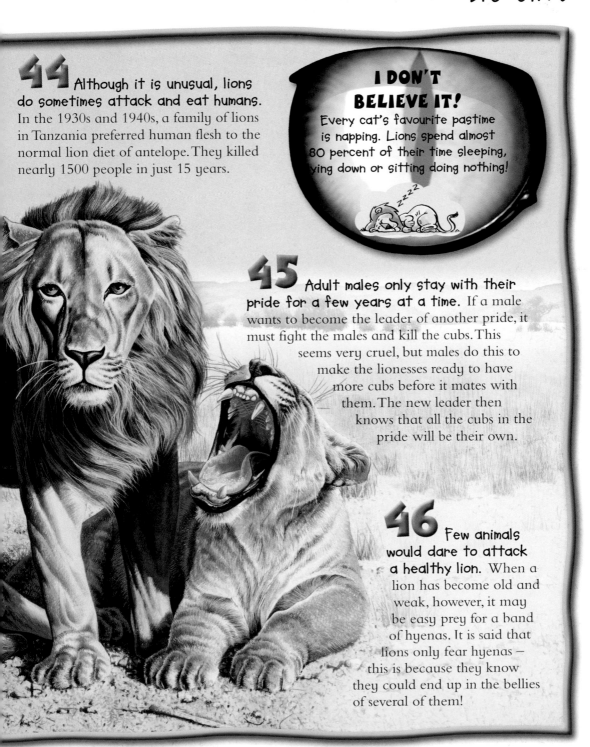

44 Although it is unusual, lions do sometimes attack and eat humans. In the 1930s and 1940s, a family of lions in Tanzania preferred human flesh to the normal lion diet of antelope. They killed nearly 1500 people in just 15 years.

I DON'T BELIEVE IT!
Every cat's favourite pastime is napping. Lions spend almost 80 percent of their time sleeping, lying down or sitting doing nothing!

45 Adult males only stay with their pride for a few years at a time. If a male wants to become the leader of another pride, it must fight the males and kill the cubs. This seems very cruel, but males do this to make the lionesses ready to have more cubs before it mates with them. The new leader then knows that all the cubs in the pride will be their own.

46 Few animals would dare to attack a healthy lion. When a lion has become old and weak, however, it may be easy prey for a band of hyenas. It is said that lions only fear hyenas — this is because they know they could end up in the bellies of several of them!

Jungle cats

47 **More than half of the world's wild cats live in forests and jungles.** In some of these forests, the weather remains hot and wet all year round. In others there are long dry spells, followed by periods of heavy rain. These rainy seasons are known as monsoons. Both types of forest are packed full of animal and plant life.

◀ Jaguars live in South American rainforests, but often stray onto farmland and prey on domestic cattle.

▼ Tigers prefer wet habitats and they are strong swimmers.

48 Tigers hide in tall grass and thick vegetation. As the sunlight and shadows flicker on the tiger's stripy fur, it blends into the background. It moves little during the day and spends most of its time resting. As the sun fades, it creeps through the forest, its paws softly padding across the forest floor. It is looking and listening for any animal that it may catch unawares.

49 Leopards are skilful hunters. Despite this, they are becoming increasingly rare in rainforest areas due to the destruction of their habitat.

50 Some jungle areas are protected and people are not allowed to cut down the trees. These areas are called 'reserves' and are meant to provide a place where animals, including all kinds of big cats, can live safely in peace.

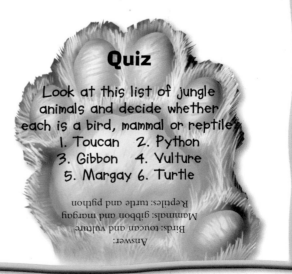

Quiz

Look at this list of jungle animals and decide whether each is a bird, mammal or reptile
1. Toucan   2. Python
3. Gibbon   4. Vulture
5. Margay 6. Turtle

Answer:
Birds: toucan and vulture
Mammals: gibbon and margay
Reptiles: turtle and python

Swift and sure

51 Big cats move in a similar way to smaller cats. They are very athletic and are able to run, climb, pounce and leap almost silently. These skills are important because when hunting they need to get as close to their prey as they can before attacking it.

▼ All cats run in a similar way. They push off with both hind legs together but land on one front foot and then the other.

Domestic cat

Cheetah

Quiz

Can you link each bone to its important job?

1. Skull 2. Ribs 3. Spine

a) Contains the nerves
b) Protects the heart
c) Protects the brain

Answers:
1.c 2.b 3.a

52 Cheetahs are the fastest of all cats. Their spines, or backbones, are so bendy they can bring their hind legs forward between their front paws when they run. This means that they can take huge steps as they bound forwards. Unlike most cats, they do not have retractable claws on their feet. When they run their claws stick into the ground like the spikes on an athlete's shoes.

53 Some cats, such as leopards, spend a lot of their time in trees. Long tails help them to keep their balance as they move along narrow branches. They can chase monkeys high up into a tree, keeping their footing on branches that seem too flimsy to support a squirrel! If the monkey falls the leopard will turn and race headfirst down the tree to reach its prey.

1. The caracal may lose its footing as it chases prey along branches

▶ When tree-climbing cats like caracals fall from a height they can usually regain their balance and land on their feet.

2. It has a superb sense of balance and quickly begins to right itself

3. A flexible spine helps the falling caracal twist its body

4. Cats' muscles are strong and their joints are very flexible so the caracal can absorb the shock of hitting the ground to give it a 'soft landing'

54 Do cats really have nine lives? It often seems that cats can survive almost any scrape they get themselves into. They don't have nine lives but their strength and quick reactions can save their lives. When a cat falls out of a tree, it can twist its body round so that it lands on its feet – and walk away with its head held high and a flick of its tail!

American athlete

▲ Pumas live in the New World, from the southern tip of South America all the way to Alaska.

55 **The puma is a great athlete.** Pumas have long hind legs packed with muscles – ideal for jumping, running and climbing. Of all the big cats, these are the most graceful. They can spring 2 metres into a tree, then bound up a further 18 metres before leaping down to the ground.

56 **Pumas are known by a variety of names.** These include cougar, panther, red jaguar, mountain screamer, catamount, deer tiger and mountain lion. People from Central and South America call them *chimblea*, *miztil*, *pagi* or *leopardo*.

I DON'T BELIEVE IT!
Though large in size, the puma is not one of the seven species of 'big cats', so it cannot roar. Instead, it makes an ear-piercing scream which scares both humans and animals alike!

screeeech!

57 **When you live in a hot climate and are covered in a coat of fur, it can be difficult to keep cool.** Pumas, like other cats, pant to lose heat. When an animal pants, it opens its mouth and lets its tongue hang out. This means that water can evaporate off the surface of the tongue, lowering the animal's body temperature.

58 Rabbits, mice, rats and hares are popular prey for pumas. They will also attack larger mammals, including deer, cattle and elks. In some places, humans have built houses in or near the pumas' natural habitat. This has resulted in people being attacked – even killed – by these wild animals. Now, people are beginning to realize that they have to respect the pumas' natural instincts and stay away from their territory.

59 These big cats are highly skilled killers. They hunt by slowly creeping up on an unsuspecting victim. When ready, they pounce, knocking their prey to the ground in one sudden hit. A single, swift bite kills the puma's victim immediately.

▼ Pumas often hunt small animals, such as hares, squirrels, beavers and turkeys.

60 Although pumas can kill porcupines, it is not an easy task. They need to flip the prickly creature onto its back before biting its soft belly. If the porcupine manages to spear the puma with one of its many spines, the wound may prove fatal.

◄ The North American porcupine can climb trees and has a crest of long spines, or quills, on its head and back.

Life in a cold climate

61 **There are no wild cats living in the Antarctic.** Maybe the weather is too cold for them or there are too few animals to eat. Some big cats do live in cold climates. Like all animals that live in these remote areas, they grow thick fur and store extra layers of fat under their skin to keep warm.

62 **The beautiful snow leopard lives in one of the most challenging habitats in the world.** It roams a mountainous area of Central Asia where the weather is cold and few plants are able to grow. Snow leopards live alone and travel across a huge area in search of food.

I DON'T BELIEVE IT!
While Siberian tigers survive winters at temperatures as low as −33°C, Bengal tigers try to keep cool in hot forests where temperatures can reach a sweltering 38°C!

63 Snow leopards hunt yaks, asses, sheep and goats as well as smaller mammals and birds. They survive the extreme cold because they have very thick fur, especially in winter. They also wrap their long tails around their bodies when they sleep to keep in heat. A snow leopard's grey coat helps to camouflage it in snow. During the summer, snow leopards often take a dip in mountain streams to cool themselves down.

64 Siberian tigers live in cold climates in Russia and China. Their coats are pale with brown stripes, rather than the more common black stripes. During the winter months their fur grows long, thick and shaggy to help keep them warm. They hunt other creatures that live in this harsh climate, such as wild boar, moose, sika deer and bears.

▼ Despite its name, the snow leopard is quite different from other leopards. It is smaller and its coat is much paler and thicker.

Super senses

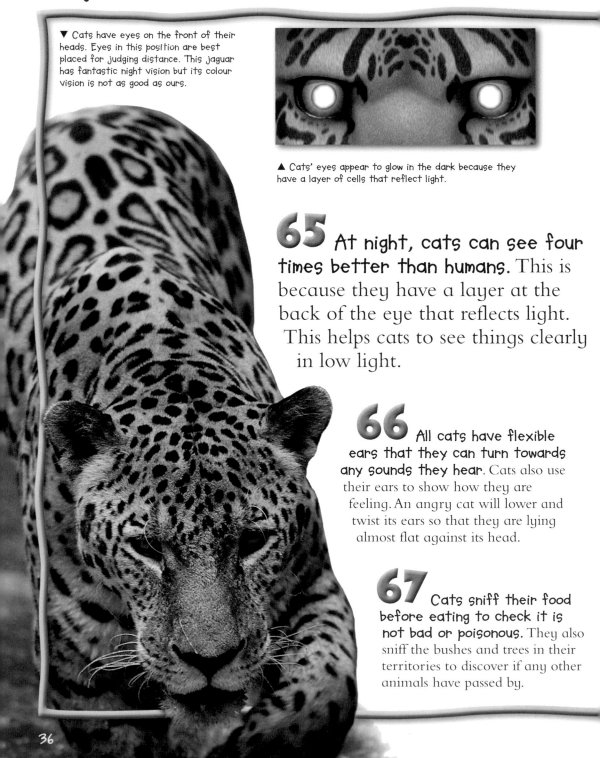

▼ Cats have eyes on the front of their heads. Eyes in this position are best placed for judging distance. This jaguar has fantastic night vision but its colour vision is not as good as ours.

▲ Cats' eyes appear to glow in the dark because they have a layer of cells that reflect light.

65 At night, cats can see four times better than humans. This is because they have a layer at the back of the eye that reflects light. This helps cats to see things clearly in low light.

66 All cats have flexible ears that they can turn towards any sounds they hear. Cats also use their ears to show how they are feeling. An angry cat will lower and twist its ears so that they are lying almost flat against its head.

67 Cats sniff their food before eating to check it is not bad or poisonous. They also sniff the bushes and trees in their territories to discover if any other animals have passed by.

▶ Clouded leopards use their whiskers to help them find their way through dense jungle vegetation, especially at night.

68 A cat's whiskers are special hairs that are extra-sensitive. They are particularly useful at night when cats are likely to be hunting. As the cat moves through undergrowth, its whiskers brush against the leaves, helping it choose a safe path. It is only by using all of their senses together that cats are able to move about easily in darkness.

▼ Despite their doglike appearance hyenas are more closely related to cats than dogs.

69 Cats use all of their senses to stay alive. As hunters, they need to be able to find, chase and catch their prey. Although big cats do not have many natural enemies, they need to watch out for scavengers, such as hyenas. These animals gang up on big cats and steal their meals.

A coat to die for

70 The jaguar is the owner of a beautiful fur coat – so beautiful that many people want to own it too. Although it is against the law to capture a jaguar for its skin, they are still hunted. Jaguars live in rainforests, often in areas where farmers are cutting back trees to grow crops. As jaguars' habitats continue to shrink, so will their numbers.

71 At first glance a jaguar looks like a leopard, but it is possible to tell them apart by a few tell-tale differences. A jaguar's head is bigger and rounder than a leopard's, with round ears not pointed ones. Its tail is quite a bit shorter than the leopards and its shoulders are broad and packed with muscle.

72 Of all the big cats jaguars are the most water-loving. They like swampy areas, or places that flood during wet seasons. Jaguars are strong swimmers and seem to enjoy bathing in rivers. They live in Central and South America but less than one hundred years ago, they were living as far north as California and Texas.

▼ Jaguars are similar to leopards but they have broader shoulders, shorter legs and larger heads. All jaguars love water.

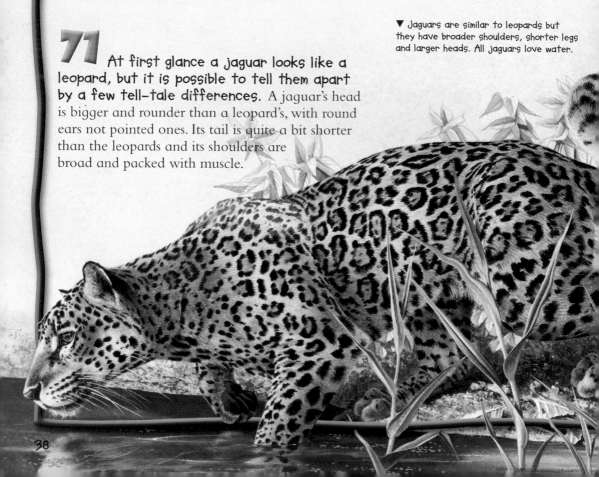

73 Young jaguars climb trees where they hunt for birds and small mammals. As they grow bigger they become too heavy for the branches. Adults tend to stay on the ground, or in water, to hunt.

▲ A capybara's eyes, ears and nose are on the top of its head so that it can spot a lurking predator as it wallows in water.

74 Jaguars hunt a wide range of animals including deer, tapirs, birds, fish and capybaras. Capybaras are the world's heaviest rodent and can measure up to 130 centimetres in length.

◄ Jaguars can feed on turtles because they have large, heavy teeth and immensely powerful jaws.

I DON'T BELIEVE IT!

In one year alone, at least 13,500 jaguars were killed for their coats. Today, the future of the jaguar is most at risk from the destruction of its rainforest habitat.

75 Jaguars' powerful jaws are so strong that they can crack open the hard shells of turtles and tortoises. These cats will even kill large animals, such as cattle and horses. It is their habit of killing cows that upsets many people who share the jaguars' territory. Cattle are very important to the farmers, who may poison or shoot jaguars that are killing their livestock.

Spots and stripes

Tiger fur

Cheetah fur

▲ The top layer of a cat's coat is made of coarse, long hair. It is this hair that is coloured and carries the pattern.

76 Patterned fur has helped cats survive, but it may be the death of them. For centuries, people have hunted cats for their beautiful coats. In some cases this has brought big cats to the edge of extinction.

77 A cat's fur keeps it warm when the weather is cold and cool when it is too hot. The fur is made up of two layers – a short and fluffy bottom layer and a top layer that is made of longer coloured fur.

▼ No one really knows why a lion's coat is generally plain tawny, while cheetahs and leopards, which live in similar habitats in Africa, are spotted. This lion's coat enables it to almost disappear into the long grass.

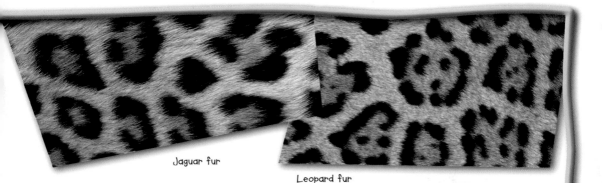

Jaguar fur

Leopard fur

Guard hairs

Underfur

Skin

◄ The layer of soft, downy fur next to a cat's skin traps air and helps to keep the cat warm.

78 **The pattern on a cat's coat helps it to blend in with its surroundings.** This is called camouflage. Spots blend in with the effect of dappled sunlight, stripes with long grasses.

▼ White patches are clearly visible on the backs of this tiger's ears.

79 **Many big cats have white patches on their ears.** This may help cubs to follow their mother in dark forest. Cats that are angry or scared usually flatten their ears and twist them so that the patches can be seen from the front. This may warn other cats to stay away.

Supercat

▲ There are probably more leopards in the wild than all the other big cats put together. This success has earned leopards the nickname 'supercat'.

80 Leopards can live close to humans but never be seen by them. They live in Africa and as far east as Malaysia, China and Korea. Leopards hunt by night and sleep in the day. They are possibly the most common of all the big cats, but are rarely seen in the wild.

81 Leopards may sit in the branches of a tree, waiting patiently for their meal to come to them. As their prey strolls past, the leopard drops from the branches and silently, quickly, kills its victim.

82 Leopards nearly always hunt at night. A leopard approaches its prey in absolute silence, making sure that it does not snap a twig or rustle leaves. With incredible control, it places its hind paws onto the exact places where its forepaws had safely rested. When it is within striking distance of its victim it will attack.

83 Leopards are not fussy eaters. They will eat dung beetles, frogs or birds if nothing better comes along. They prefer to hunt monkeys, pigs and antelopes.

◀ Dung beetles feed on dung and lay their eggs in it. They make a crunchy snack for hungry leopards.

84 Once a leopard has caught its meal, it does not want to lose it to passing scavengers such as hyenas or jackals. The leopard might climb up a tree, hauling its prey with it. It may choose to eat immediately or store the animal for later. Hiding food like this is called 'caching' (known as 'cashing').

85 Although the name 'panther' is usually given to pumas, it is also used for leopards that have black fur. Black panthers are not a different type of leopard – some cubs are simply born with black fur rather than the normal tawny-brown hide.

◀ If you could get close enough to a black panther you would see that its fur is spotted.

Scaredy cat

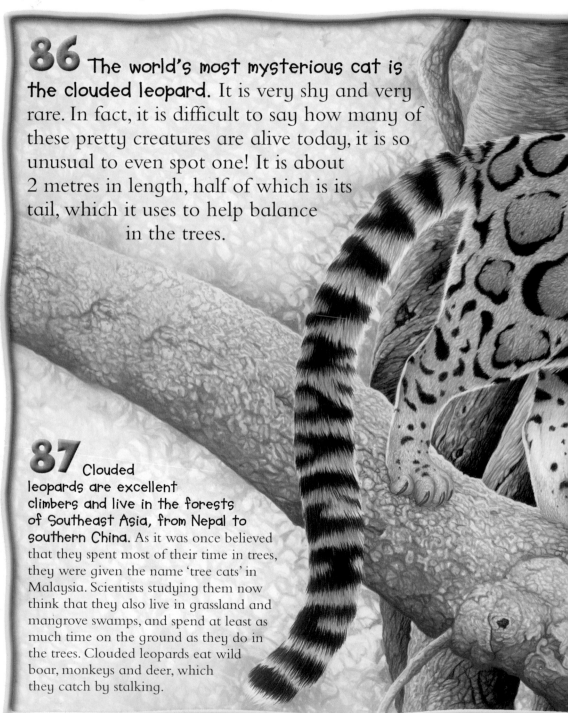

86 The world's most mysterious cat is the clouded leopard. It is very shy and very rare. In fact, it is difficult to say how many of these pretty creatures are alive today, it is so unusual to even spot one! It is about 2 metres in length, half of which is its tail, which it uses to help balance in the trees.

87 Clouded leopards are excellent climbers and live in the forests of Southeast Asia, from Nepal to southern China. As it was once believed that they spent most of their time in trees, they were given the name 'tree cats' in Malaysia. Scientists studying them now think that they also live in grassland and mangrove swamps, and spend at least as much time on the ground as they do in the trees. Clouded leopards eat wild boar, monkeys and deer, which they catch by stalking.

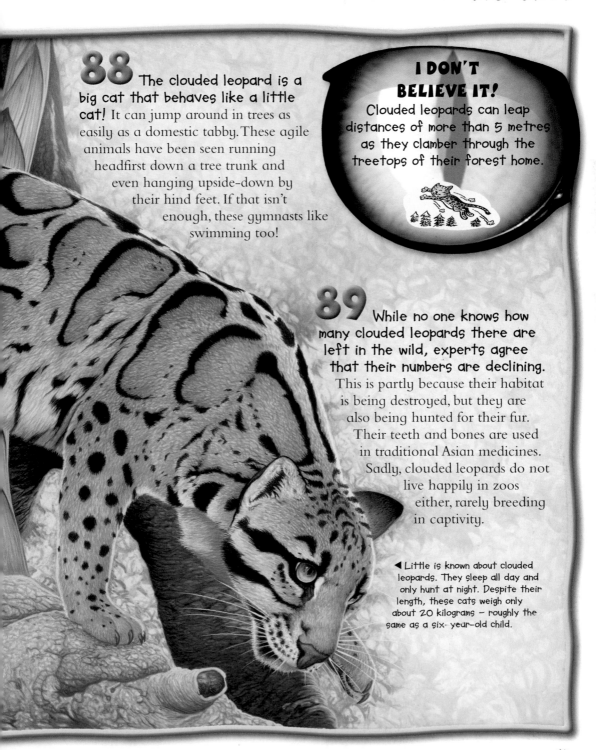

88 The clouded leopard is a big cat that behaves like a little cat! It can jump around in trees as easily as a domestic tabby. These agile animals have been seen running headfirst down a tree trunk and even hanging upside-down by their hind feet. If that isn't enough, these gymnasts like swimming too!

I DON'T BELIEVE IT!
Clouded leopards can leap distances of more than 5 metres as they clamber through the treetops of their forest home.

89 While no one knows how many clouded leopards there are left in the wild, experts agree that their numbers are declining. This is partly because their habitat is being destroyed, but they are also being hunted for their fur. Their teeth and bones are used in traditional Asian medicines. Sadly, clouded leopards do not live happily in zoos either, rarely breeding in captivity.

◀ Little is known about clouded leopards. They sleep all day and only hunt at night. Despite their length, these cats weigh only about 20 kilograms – roughly the same as a six- year-old child.

45

Cat cousins

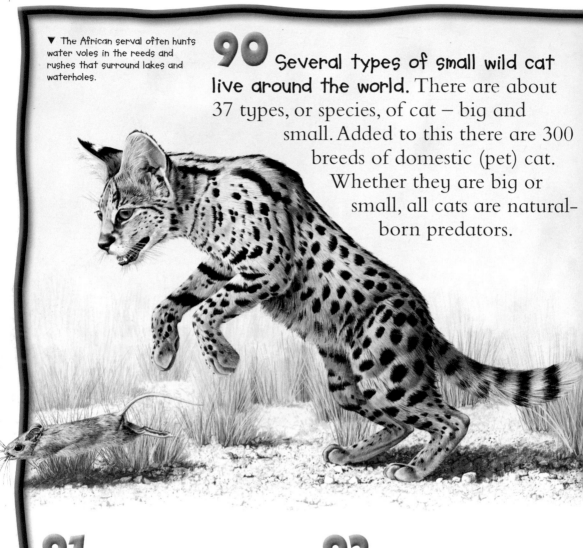

▼ The African serval often hunts water voles in the reeds and rushes that surround lakes and waterholes.

90 **Several types of small wild cat live around the world.** There are about 37 types, or species, of cat – big and small. Added to this there are 300 breeds of domestic (pet) cat. Whether they are big or small, all cats are natural-born predators.

91 **One of the world's bounciest cats is the serval.** It can leap one metre high and travel a distance of 4 metres as it jumps like a jack-in-the-box to strike at its prey. All this effort may be for a small supper of frogs or locusts, which are some of the serval's favourite titbits.

92 **The serval is unusual because it hunts during the day.** Most cats prefer to hunt at night or during the dimly-lit hours of morning or evening. Servals live in the African savannah and look very similar to cheetahs, with a slim, graceful body and long, slender forelimbs.

93 Like its neighbour the jaguar the ocelot has been hunted for its fur. It lives in the forests, grasslands and swamps of South America. Ocelots usually live alone or in pairs and will eat almost anything they can catch. Until the hunting of these extraordinary cats was made illegal, as many as 200,000 pelts (skins) were sold every year.

▶ The ocelot is extremely agile and can leap from the ground on a dark night and grab a low-flying bat in its paws or mouth.

94 The lynx can change its coat according to the weather. In fact its winter coat looks so different from its summer one that you might not think it was the same animal! This cat lives in pine forests across northern Europe and Asia. All year round, it has a short tail and tufts of fur on the tip of each ear. It can kill animals four times bigger than itself.

95 One super-springy cat is the caracal. It can leap an astonishing 3 metres into the air to swipe at a passing bird! A long time ago, this fine hunter was trained to catch birds and hares in India and Iran. Caracals live in dry, scrubby habitats which is why they have another name: the desert lynx.

◀ Wide, furry paws help prevent a lynx from sinking into the snow and give it a good grip on icy rocks.

A race against time

▲ When rainforests are cut down, millions of animals lose their homes.

96 Most of the big cats featured in this book are threatened with extinction. That means that they could disappear completely from the wild in the near future. One of the main reasons for this is the destruction of the big cats' habitat. All over the world, people and animals are fighting for space. Predators need plenty of space to hunt, but people need land to grow crops and graze cattle. Large areas of forest are also cut down to sell the trees or to search for valuable minerals underground.

I DON'T BELIEVE IT!
It is too late for some big cats. The Taiwan clouded leopard, the Caspian, Bali and Javan tigers are extinct. There are only about 260 Asiatic lions left in the wild.

97 It is the misfortune of many big cats that they have wonderful fur. For the last few hundred years, cats have been killed in their hundreds of thousands so that people can wear their skins. Most of this hunting is now against the law, but it still continues. Farmers also kill big cats that steal their cattle and other animals. These people need their animals to feed their families, or to sell to make money.

98 Wherever possible, zoos and wildlife parks keep big cats safe. Scientists help the animals to breed in the hope that one day they can be returned to the wild. However, it is not an easy task. Cheetahs and clouded leopards, for example, are very difficult to breed.

99 The Iberian lynx, which only lives in Spain and Portugal, is considered the most endangered of all the larger cats. It is now fully protected by law, but its habitat is so tiny that it doesn't have much chance of survival in the wild.

▲ The beautiful Iberian lynx mostly eats rabbits, deer and ducks. Cubs are usually born in April and stay with their mother until the following spring.

▼ Not long ago, people shot lions with guns. Now tourists come to Africa to shoot close-up photographs of big cats in their natural habitat.

100 The best way to shoot a big cat is through a camera lens. Tourists will pay a lot of money if they are promised the sight of a big cat. Now, in many places, the local people are doing everything they can to look after their wildlife so they can share it with visitors who come to their country.

Masters of the forest

101 **In the snowy lands surrounding the Arctic, bears used to be known as 'masters of the forest'.** Bears are some of the largest creatures to live on land and they have few natural enemies, except humans. Once they roamed many of the planet's forests, but now these magnificent animals face an uncertain future.

▶ Brown bears eat a lot of fish and often wait at rivers and waterfalls for salmon. They catch the fish in their powerful jaws, or hook them out of the water with their huge paws, but they have to be quick!

What is a bear?

102 There are eight types, or species, of bear including polar bears, grizzly bears and giant pandas. All have large, heavy bodies, big heads and short, powerful legs.

▼ An angry bear may roar, opening its powerful jaw to reveal massive teeth.

103 Most bears are brown in colour. Polar bears have white, or yellow-white coats, which help them blend into their snowy Arctic habitat. Pandas have striking black-and-white markings. Bears have thick fur, which helps to keep them warm – and makes them look even bigger than they actually are.

104 When they show their teeth and growl, bears are a scary sight. They belong to a group of meat-eating creatures called carnivores. The large, sharp teeth at the front of their mouths are called canines, and they use them for stabbing and tearing at meat. These teeth may measure between 5 and 8 centimetres in length.

105 A close look at a bear reveals that its eyes are actually quite small compared to the size of its head. Bears have good eyesight, but their sense of smell is much stronger. They can even smell food hidden in a glove compartment, inside a locked car!

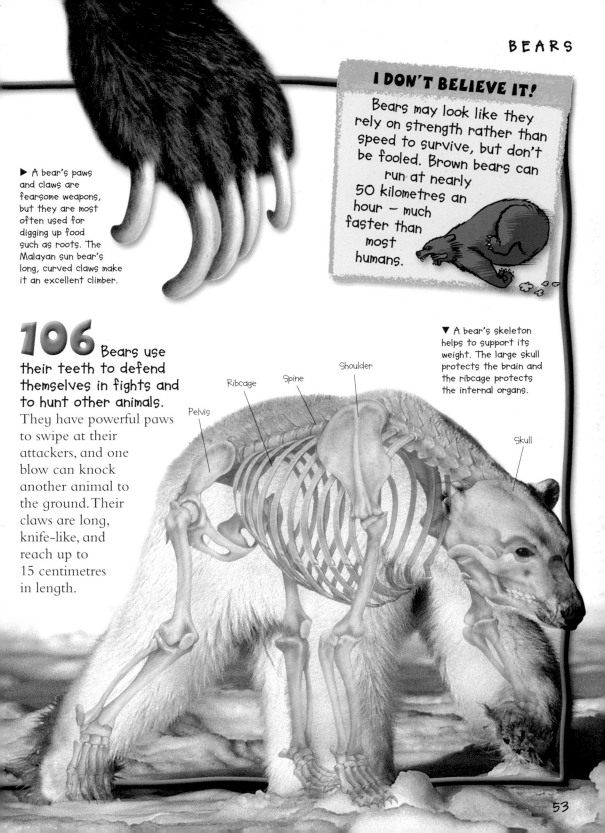

► A bear's paws and claws are fearsome weapons, but they are most often used for digging up food such as roots. The Malayan sun bear's long, curved claws make it an excellent climber.

I DON'T BELIEVE IT!

Bears may look like they rely on strength rather than speed to survive, but don't be fooled. Brown bears can run at nearly 50 kilometres an hour – much faster than most humans.

106 Bears use their teeth to defend themselves in fights and to hunt other animals. They have powerful paws to swipe at their attackers, and one blow can knock another animal to the ground. Their claws are long, knife-like, and reach up to 15 centimetres in length.

▼ A bear's skeleton helps to support its weight. The large skull protects the brain and the ribcage protects the internal organs.

Pelvis

Ribcage

Spine

Shoulder

Skull

Habits and homes

107 Today, most bear species are rare. They are still found in areas of the Arctic, the Americas, Europe and Asia, but once, bears lived in woodlands all over the world.

108 Bears can live in a variety of places, from the icy north to the hot forests of South-east Asia. Sloth bears can even live in dry scrubland as long as ants and honey are available. Despite their size, most bears can climb trees.

109 Although they are carnivores, bears often have to settle for a snack of leaves, roots and fruits. The polar bear eats only meat, because there are almost no plants in the Arctic, but other bears rely on plants for the bulk of their diet. Since plants don't contain as much energy-rich fat as meat, most bears have to spend lots of their time eating and searching for food.

▼ Bears like the sweet taste of ripe berries and feast on these in the autumn.

▲ Brown bears spend the winter sleeping in rocky caves lined with leaves and grass.

110 Bears are solitary animals – they prefer to live alone. Mothers and cubs make small families, but once they have grown, young bears head off on their own to face the world by themselves.

111 Bears make the most of the summer and autumn months, when there is more food around, to eat and gain weight. When winter comes, bears that live in cool or cold climates retreat to their dens and sleep through the worst weather. They need big stores of body fat to help them survive during this time as they may not eat for many months.

▶ A bear family stays close together for safety. The cubs are at risk of being hunted by other meat eaters, including other bears.

Bears from the past

112 *Arctodus* was the biggest bear to have ever lived. It lived around the time of the last Ice Age, becoming extinct about 11,500 years ago. Known as the giant short-faced bear, it was over 3 metres in height when standing up on its back legs. The spectacled bears that live in South America today may be related to *Arctodus*.

◀ Fearsome *Arctodus* defends its kill from Ice Age wolves.

▲ Humans called Neanderthals hunted cave bears for meat, and used their bones and teeth as ornaments.

Meet my family

Who are your relatives — and where do you come from?

Ask your parents and grandparents about the people in your family, where they came from and what they did with their lives. There may be old family photos or letters you could look at together.

115 Cave bears were hunted by early humans, and this may have contributed to them dying out. They may also have found it hard to survive in the cold climate. The ground was covered in snow and ice for much of the year, and food would have been scarce.

113 Today's bears are thought to be descended from *Ursavus*, a bear that lived 20 to 15 million years ago. Also called the dawn bear, it was the size of a small dog, and lived in Europe when the climate was hot and humid, like today's tropics. It was millions of years before more bearlike creatures evolved.

116 Atlas bears were common in North Africa, until the Romans started capturing them in the 6th century. The bears, along with elephants and lions, were killed in arenas for entertainment. In a single day 100 bears could be killed, and numbers of wild Atlas bears fell dramatically. The last Atlas bears died around 140 years ago.

114 Giant cave bears were common in Europe during the Ice Age. Scientists have learnt about cave bears from the remains of teeth and bones they have found. They were similar to brown bears but were bigger and ate plants.

Curious cousins

117 There may only be eight species of bear, but other animals exist that are similar. In fact for many years, scientists thought that sloth bears were actually sloths (which is how they got their name) and that giant pandas were a type of raccoon! Some of these lookalikes are actually related to bears, but some just share their characteristics or life-style.

▼ Their appearance and behaviour may be very different, but walruses probably share the same ancestor as bears.

I DON'T BELIEVE IT!

Koalas eat eucalyptus leaves, which contain poisons that their bodies are able to remove. They don't need to drink water — and their name is an Aboriginal word meaning 'no drink'!

118 Bears are related to a family of animals called **pinnipeds.** These are mammals that live in the sea and come ashore mainly to breed. Examples of pinnipeds include seals, sea lions and walruses. Despite the fact that these creatures look completely different to bears, scientists have discovered that pinnipeds and bears probably shared a common ancestor, which lived around 30 million years ago.

◄ Red pandas look similar to raccoons, with bushy, striped tails, but they have red backs and black legs and bellies. They live similar lives to giant pandas, but are not bears.

119 Like giant pandas, red (lesser) pandas live in mountainous forests of China. They spend more time in trees than giant pandas and climb to escape predators or to sunbathe. They feed mainly on the ground, eating bamboo shoots, roots, fruit and small animals.

120 Bear cats are not bears or cats! Also known as binturongs, these stocky tree-climbers live in the tropical rainforests of south and south-eastern Asia. They have shaggy black fur and long gripping tails and will eat whatever food they can find, including fruit and birds.

121 Koalas are often called 'koala bears' but they are not related to bears at all. They are marsupials, which means they give birth to undeveloped young that are then protected in a pouch as they grow. Koalas only live in eastern Australia and feed on the leaves of eucalyptus trees.

► Koalas are similar to bears in appearance. They climb trees and have sharp claws.

Cute cubs

122 Female bears are called sows and they usually give birth to two or three babies called cubs. Sows start having cubs when they are four years old, and they may only have between eight and ten cubs in their whole lives. Adult males are called boars and they have nothing to do with rearing the youngsters.

▲ Newborn cubs are tiny and helpless. They have little or no hair, so they need to stay close to their mother for warmth. These grizzly bear cubs are just 10 days old.

123 They may have large parents, but bear cubs are very small. A giant panda cub weighs as little as 90 grams when it is born, and is easily hidden by its mother's paw. Cubs are born with their eyes and ears closed, and their bodies are either completely naked, or covered with a fine layer of soft fur. Like all mammals, female bears feed their young on milk, which is produced by the mother's body. For the first few months, cubs feed often and soon build up their strength.

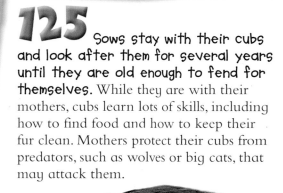

125 Sows stay with their cubs and look after them for several years until they are old enough to fend for themselves. While they are with their mothers, cubs learn lots of skills, including how to find food and how to keep their fur clean. Mothers protect their cubs from predators, such as wolves or big cats, that may attack them.

124 Female bears give birth to their cubs in dens that they have prepared. They usually make their dens by digging into the soil, often under large stones or around tree roots. They line the den with dry plants and may use the same den for several winters. Polar bear mothers have to make their dens in snow and ice.

▶ Bears are mammals, like cats, dogs and humans, and females feed their young with milk that is produced by their bodies.

Black bears

126 Areas of North America and Canada are home to black bears. They live in mountains and forests, and despite being very shy, they sometimes stray into towns. They avoid brown bears, which also live in the American continent.

127 Most black bears are black, but some have brown or even white fur. Dark-furred black bears sometimes have lighter fur on their muzzles (noses) and chests. Their long, curved claws help them grip tree trunks when climbing trees.

True or false?

1. A muzzle is the name given to some animals' long noses.
2. Black bears live in Europe.
3. 'Scavenge' means finding scraps and waste food.
4. A carnivore eats meat.

Answers:
1.True 2. False 3. True 4.True

128 These big bears need to eat plenty of food to keep their energy levels high. During the summer they mostly eat plants, but the actual food they eat depends on where they live, the time of the year and what is available. Black bears rarely hunt other animals, although they eat insects such as beetles, and love honey.

129 Black bears are regarded as the most intelligent of all bears. Those that live near humans often use their sense of smell to locate rubbish bins. They find ways to break into the bins and rifle through piles of garbage. Black bears are often found in national parks where they wander into campsites in search of food, particularly at night.

130 Thousands of black bears are killed by humans every year. Only one out of every ten black bears dies naturally. The others are all killed by hunters, or after being hit by cars. Yet black bears manage to survive and are not in danger of becoming extinct.

◄ Black bears avoid humans, and if they see people they are much more likely to run away or climb up a tree than attack.

Surviving the winter

131 **Most black bears live in places where winters are very cold.** This is a difficult time as food is scarce, and they survive by having a long winter sleep. This is called 'hibernating', and other bears that live in cold climates hibernate too.

▼ When snow and ice settle on the ground, black bears hide away. Female black bears look after their cubs in dens lined with grass and leaves.

132 **During hibernation, a black bear's body systems slow down.** Its body temperature drops and its heart beats much more slowly – dropping from 40 to 50 beats to just 8 beats per minute! Unlike other hibernating animals, bears often wake up to clean themselves and get comfortable.

▲ Black bear cubs stay with their mothers for two to three years. A cub learns to hunt by watching and copying everything its mother does.

133 **Pregnant females that are hibernating give birth in January or February.** Sows look after their helpless cubs in their cosy dens until the spring arrives. They then leave their dens to hunt because after a long winter hibernating they are starving. During this time, sows prefer to eat meat rather than plants, as it is a good source of protein, so they can quickly build up their strength. They catch young animals that have been born in the spring, such as deer fawns, beaver kits and moose calves.

134 **Some black bears have white fur!** The kermode, or spirit, bear has a creamy-white coat and white claws, but is otherwise the same as an American black bear. They can have black or white cubs.

135 **Black bears may spend most of the winter asleep, but they enjoy long naps in the summer too!** They are most active in the early mornings and late evenings but during the hot daytime they often sneak under vegetation (plants) to sleep in the cooler shadows.

Polar bears

136 The polar bear is the biggest type of bear, and the largest meat-eating animal on Earth. These huge beasts have to fight to survive in one of the planet's bleakest places.

137 The Arctic is a snow-and-ice-covered region around the North Pole. Temperatures are record-breaking, dropping to an incredible -70°C and, unsurprisingly, very few living things are found there. Polar bears, however, manage to cope with howling winds, freezing snow blizzards and long winters.

I DON'T BELIEVE IT!

The word 'Arctic' comes from the Greek word 'Arkitos', which means country of the Great Bear. This doesn't refer to polar bears though, but to the Great Bear constellation, or pattern of stars, in the sky.

138 Polar bears are covered in a thick layer of white fur. This helps them to stay warm because it keeps in their body heat, and even absorbs some of the Sun's warming energy. Each hair is a colourless hollow tube which appears white when it reflects light. Some bears have yellow fur, especially in the summer when they spend less time in water and their coats get dirty.

139 Polar bears also have a layer of fat called blubber beneath the skin, which traps in heat. This is where the bears store energy for the months when they may not be able to find food. The blubber may be up to 12 centimetres thick and is so effective at helping the bear stay warm that polar bears are more likely to get too hot than too cold!

140 Female polar bears spend the winter months in dens so their cubs can be born safely. A mother spends five or six months in the snug den with her cubs, while the bad winter weather rages outside. She doesn't eat or drink during all of this time, but survives on her body fat.

◀ The Arctic summer is short, so polar bears like to soak up the sunshine in between hunting trips. Young cubs stay close to their mother at all times.

Life in the cold

141 The Arctic may be a difficult place in which to survive, but the seas and oceans around it are full of life. The huge number of fish attracts seals to these areas – and they are the main part of a polar bear's diet, especially ringed seals.

▶ Polar bears have been known to wait by a seal's breathing hole for hours, even days. When the time is right, they lunge forwards to catch their prey.

142 Unlike most other bears, polar bears don't have a home range (territory) that they stay in. The Arctic ice continually melts, refreezes and moves, changing the landscape throughout the year. Polar bears have to keep on the move and search for food. Their diets are 'fast and feast', meaning they may not eat for weeks, but when they find food they eat lots of it.

143 Seals are mammals and need to breathe air. They spend much of their time under water hunting fish, but they have to come up to the surface from time to time. Seals make themselves air holes in the ice and polar bears sit patiently, waiting for an unsuspecting seal to poke its head out of the water.

◀ A single swipe from a powerful polar bear's paw is enough to kill a seal.

144

With lightning reactions, a polar bear can lunge at a seal, whacking it with a powerful paw or grasping it in its enormous jaws. It then drags the seal away from the hole before tucking in. Polar bears have to spend around half their time hunting.

145

Polar bears are excellent swimmers and often take to the water to get from one iceberg to another. They can swim at speeds of 10 kilometres an hour using their paws to paddle through the crystal clear seas of the Arctic. They can dive underwater and hold their breath for up to 2 minutes.

▼ Polar bears' bodies are well suited to the water. When a polar bear dives, its thick layer of body fat keeps it warm and its nostrils close against the icy water.

Brown bears

146 **The mighty brown bear is a massive, shaggy-haired beast that lives in the northern parts of the world.** Long ago, brown bears were spread far and wide across the world, but now they are finding it difficult to survive in places where they come into contact with humans.

147 **Brown bears are now mostly found in forests, mountains and scrubland, in remote places where few people roam.** There are brown bears in Northern Europe, Siberia, Asia, Alaska, Canada and parts of the United States. Bears from different areas can look quite different from one another. They vary in colour from yellowish to almost black.

148 **Kodiak bears are the largest of all brown bears and can weigh up to 800 kilograms.** They stand almost twice as high as a human. Their size is due to their diet – these big animals eat lots of fish, which is packed with healthy fats and proteins. Kodiak bears live on Kodiak Island, in Alaska, North America.

◄ A brown bear can reach 3 metres in length and normally weighs between 200 and 600 kilograms. They rub up against trees to scratch their backs.

150 Brown bears may be huge animals, but they can run with speed if they need to. Their walking looks slow and lumbering, but a scared bear can change pace very quickly — and run faster than most other animals.

149 Brown bears live in northern areas where it is very cold in winter, so they usually hibernate. Some types spend up to seven months in a den, but all bears wake up occasionally. When they wake they rearrange their bedding, clean themselves and return to sleep.

▶ Male bears are called boars and may sometimes fight one another using jaws, paws and claws.

151 Grizzlies are the famous brown bears of North America. They once roamed as far south as Mexico, but now they live in western Canada and Alaska. They get their name from the white hairs that grow in their brown coats, giving them a grizzled appearance.

71

Gone hunting

152 Grizzlies spend hours wading in water, or standing on a river's edge watching and waiting for salmon. During the summer and autumn, salmon swim upstream to lay their eggs, and as the fish swim past, the bears pounce on them.

153 With a single blow from its large paw, a bear can easily stun a fish. Grizzlies can also catch their prey in their mouths, delivering a quick and fatal bite with their enormous teeth. Grizzlies are good swimmers, and will even dive underwater to catch salmon swimming past them.

▲ Grizzlies usually hunt and kill their prey, but they will also eat animal remains that have been abandoned by other hunters.

154 Bears eat almost anything, from berries, shoots and roots to insects, fish and small mammals. Sometimes they hunt and attack living animals, especially young elks or caribou deer. They also eat carrion – the dead remains of animals killed by other predators, or hunters, such as wolves, coyotes and other bears.

◀ A grizzly chases a salmon through the water. Salmon are highly nutritious, so brown bears that hunt them often grow bigger than other brown bears.

▼ Grizzlies stand and wait for salmon to leap out of the water. Like other brown bears, they have distinctive humps on their shoulders.

156 Grizzlies inspired the first teddy bear, which appeared around 100 years ago. Teddies were named after an American president called Teddy Roosevelt, who refused to shoot a grizzly on a hunting trip. The story was in a newspaper and a toyshop owner decided to make a stuffed bear — and called it a teddy.

155 Grizzlies may travel long distances in search of food, but they usually return to their territory. Bears are sometimes trapped and moved to other areas by scientists and wildlife managers to keep them away from humans, but a few have been able to find their way home — up to 200 kilometres away. No one knows how they do this, but their great sense of smell may help.

My Home

Do you know where you live? Ask a grown up to help you find your street on a map of your area, and then find your school. Can you trace the route home from your school, following the roads? Then use a big atlas and find your country on a map of the world.

73

Moon bears

▲ Moon bears often eat farmers' crops such as maize (sweetcorn). They visit the fields and tear off the maize cobs using their long teeth called canines. This is why they are often trapped or hunted.

158 Moon bears spend a lot of time in trees, sleeping or searching for nuts, leaves and fruit. They live in forested areas and are most active at night. Very little is known about how these animals behave in the wild.

159 These bears rely on their sense of smell more than sight or sound. They rub against trees, leaving a strong scent to warn other bears to stay out of their territory. Moon bears can be very aggressive if they encounter humans – they are more likely than an American black bear to kill a person, despite being smaller.

157 Moon bears are black bears of Asia and they have white or cream patches of fur on their chests. These patches of fur are often shaped like crescent moons – which is how they get their name. They are also known as Asiatic black bears.

Moon bears build themselves nests up in trees, rather like birds! They make platforms from branches and plants and sleep in them at night, safe from danger.

▲ Some moon bears are kept in cramped cages so people can remove a fluid called bile that their bodies naturally create. Bile is an ingredient in some medicines. Many organizations are trying to bring this cruel practice to an end.

160 **The moon bear can stand, and even walk, on its back feet.** This skill led to many of these creatures being taken from the wild when they were still cubs. They were brought to circuses, where they were trained to 'dance' for the crowds.

161 **Moon bears are threatened with extinction because their forests have been taken over by farmers.** They are regarded as pests in many places, and many of them have been killed. In China, these bears are captured so their body parts can be used in traditional medicines.

◄ Moon bears weigh between 100 and 200 kilograms and measure up to 2 metres in length. Moon bears in captivity are able to stand up and beg for food.

Sloth bears

162 Sloth bears live in South-east Asia. They can survive in a variety of places, from forests to grasslands if they can find ants, termites and fruit to eat. A sloth bear's sense of smell is so good it can even sniff out ants in the soil beneath its feet.

▼ The claws of a sloth bear can measure 8 centimetres in length and are great for digging away at a giant termite mound.

163 When a sloth bear finds an insect nest it rips it open with its claws. They may tear the bark off a tree or dig into the ground. Once the nest is open the bear sucks up the insects. The sucking noise it makes can be heard up to 100 metres away!

◄ Sloth bears can give birth at any time of year, and the young are carried on the mother's back.

164 Sloth bear cubs can be born at any time of year, and there are normally one or two cubs in a litter. The mother protects the youngsters in her den until they are about three months old. When the cubs emerge, their mother carries them on her back until they are about nine months old.

▼ Using sloth bears as dancing bears is illegal, but it is thought that many cubs continue to be captured for this purpose. Ropes are forced through their noses and their teeth are removed. Wildlife organizations are campaigning to end this cruel practise.

165 Like other bear species, sloth bears are solitary animals, but they will sometimes gather together to share a big feast. A bees' nest full of honey or a large termite mound may attract two or more bears, but after the meal, they wander off on their own again.

166 When bears stand on their hind legs they get a better view of what's going on around them. Many bears do this, not just sloth bears. Standing on their hind legs helps them to sniff scents in the air, or to look larger and more dangerous when they are feeling threatened.

Spectacled bears

167 The spectacled bear has pale fur around its eyes, so it looks as if it's wearing spectacles! It faces extinction and may not survive this century.

168 Spectacled bears are relatively small, with dense black or dark brown coats. They spend much of their time in trees, where they sleep in nests built from branches. They are most active at night and are very shy, so not much is known about them.

169 Spectacled bears are skilled climbers. They use their long, sharp claws to grip onto tree bark as they clamber up a tree, and they sometimes make nests among the branches. They can also swim, but they don't eat fish. These bears travel around the forest on four legs, but mother bears can hold their cubs in their forelimbs, and walk upright on their back legs.

◀ Scientists can recognize individual spectacled bears from the markings on their faces — every bear has a different pattern of pale fur.

170
Farmers sometimes blame these bears for eating their animals, but this is unfair. Spectacled bears eat fruit, palms and bromeliads, which are plants that have stiff, spiny leaves. They can even eat cactus plants! They do occasionally eat small mammals, such as rodents, and insects.

▼ Spectacled bears are the only bears that live in South America. In mountainous regions such as Peru, they search for plants and small animals to eat. The males are about twice the size of the females.

171
Spectacled bears don't hibernate, because they live in warm places where this isn't necessary. Mother bears still build dens for their cubs, often in tree roots or under rocks. They make unusual noises to communicate with their cubs, including screeching and soft purring sounds.

Sun bears

▲ Sun bears are also called Malay bears, dog bears and honey bears. They have very short fur and yellow patches on their chests.

172 The sun bear of South-east Asia may be the smallest of all bears, but it has the longest tongue – reaching up to 25 centimetres in length! A long tongue is very useful for reaching inside small cracks in trees and licking up tasty grubs and bugs.

173 Apart from insects, sun bears like to eat birds, lizards, fruit, honey and rodents. Their jaws are so strong they can even crack open tough coconuts to get to the edible part inside. One of their favourite foods is honey, and sun bears use their very long, curved claws to rip open hives.

175 Sun bears are the smallest bears. They are nocturnal (active at night) and shy, so no one knows how many exist. They may be the most endangered bears. In Thailand, baby sun bears are popular pets — but once they grow up they are too dangerous, and are chained up or killed.

176 Tigers and leopards hunt sun bears, but sometimes the bears wriggle free from these big cats' clutches. They have very loose, baggy skin on the backs of their necks, so if a predator attacks they can twist round and bite them!

174 In the language of Malaysia, where some sun bears live, their name means 'he who likes to sit high'. It's a perfect name for these tree-loving beasts. A sun bear uses its strong muscles, the bare skin on the soles of its feet, and its long claws when clambering up trees, and these animals can spend many hours settled in the branches of a tree eating, sleeping and sunbathing.

▶ A sun bear will tear open a bees' nest with its claws before using its long tongue to reach the sweet honey. Its tongue can stretch 25 centimetres to lick food out of cracks.

Giant pandas

177 With its distinctive white face and black eye patches there are few animals that are as easy to recognize as the giant panda. These large bears have been brought to the brink of extinction, partly by human actions.

▼ Giant pandas only live in the cool bamboo woodlands and forests in China, South Asia. These areas are often covered in snow.

178 Pandas spend a lot of time on the ground, but they climb trees to rest or sleep. Youngsters first start climbing when they are just six months old and use their claws to help them grip onto the trees. Pandas like to rest in forked branches, and watch the world beneath them. They often come down from trees head first!

179 Pandas rarely eat meat, and spend around 16 hours a day chewing bamboo. This is a tough grass-like plant that grows very tall. Pandas also eat honey, eggs, fish, and occasionally mice.

▶ When they feed, giant pandas sit with their legs outstretched in front of them.

180 Pandas have a special bone on their wrists, which grows rather like a thumb. This bone enables pandas to grab hold of clumps of bamboo in their paws, making it easier for them to collect and eat their food. Pandas have to drink fresh water regularly, so they visit streams or rivers almost every day.

▶ Pandas' forepaws are bigger than their hind paws. The forepaw has a special pad of tough skin over an extra bone, which it uses like a thumb to help it grip bamboo.

181 Pandas are not ready to mate until they are about five years old. During the mating season males sometimes fight. Females usually give birth to one or two tiny cubs that are entirely helpless. Usually, a mother only feeds the first cub that is born and leaves the other one to die.

Under threat

182 **It has been discovered that only about 1600 pandas live in the wild.** This means that despite the efforts of Chinese wildlife workers, this species of bear may become extinct everywhere except zoos in the near future.

183 **Pandas were only discovered by the western world in 1869 – but once people heard about them, they wanted to see pandas for themselves.** The bears were captured, dead or alive, and brought to zoos or museums. We are still learning about pandas and only recently found out that males do headstands by trees to spray their urine high up to mark their territory!

Panda faces

You will need:
paper plate scissors
thick black paper glue string

1. With an adult's help cut a paper plate in half.
2. Cut out eye patches, ears and a nose from the black paper and glue them on to the plate.
3. Attach string to the back if you want to hang your panda face on the wall.

184 People have taken over pandas' habitats, forcing them into smaller, more remote mountainous areas. This means that less food is available to them. They are also slow breeders — females only produce about five to eight cubs in a lifetime, and these are vulnerable to attack by predators such as leopards, martens (weasel-like creatures) and Asian wild dogs.

185 Giant pandas spend up to 16 hours a day chomping and chewing on bamboo, and they often eat during the night too. They have to spend lots of time eating because their guts lack the bacteria that help other plant eaters, such as cows, get goodness from their food. From time to time, all the bamboo in one forest may flower and then die. The pandas in the area then face starvation.

◀ Every day, pandas eat between 10 and 20 kilograms of bamboo. They have the digestive systems of meat eaters, so they need to eat huge quantities of plant matter to get enough goodness to survive.

Myths and legends

186 Bears are seen as mighty, magical and majestic creatures in many cultures. They feature in folk tales and legends throughout the world, and are feared and respected in equal amounts.

187 Bears are sometimes thought of as powerful spirits that can influence peoples' lives. Long ago, people in northern countries feared a bear spirit could control other animals, and even take them away if they upset him.

188 Berserkirs were Viking warriors who dressed themselves in bear skins and worked themselves into a trance before battle. In this state, they were wild and fearless and dangerous to anyone who got in their way. This is where the word 'berserk' comes from.

◀ Viking Berserkir warriors rushed madly into battle, wearing bear skins over their chain mail armour.

I DON'T BELIEVE IT!

Bears inspire people who want to be as strong as they are, so some sports teams are named after them. The Chicago Bears, for example, are an American football team and the Memphis Grizzlies are basketball players.

189 The Samoyed and Lapps are tribes of people who live close to the North Pole. Like other people who share their habitat with bears, they used to believe that, with the use of magic, humans could turn themselves into bears. Brave warriors were often thought to have taken on the spirits of bears as they fought.

◀ A Danish legend tells of a bear that was the king's ancestor. The bear was killed by dogs, but survives in folk tales.

190 A Danish story describes how a bear and a beautiful woman fell in love. The bear cared for her by stealing food from farms, until one day, farmers used dogs and spears to kill him. The woman later gave birth to a boy that looked normal, but was as strong and brave as a bear, who became the ancestor of the kings of Denmark.

▶ A giant armoured bear, called Iorek, features in the 2008 movie *The Golden Compass*, which is based on the book *Northern Lights*, by Philip Pullman.

Bear behaviour

191 Most bears are shy creatures and prefer to avoid coming into contact with humans. Mother bears, however, will attack any person or animal that comes too close to her cubs.

▶ When bears live near humans, they lose their fear of them and may even start to scavenge rubbish and other food.

CAUTION

ACTIVE BEARS IN AREA

PLEASE USE CAUTION WHILE WALKING:
- CARRY A BELL
- MAKE NOISE
- BE ALERT

192 Angry bears give warning signs that they may attack. These include making huffing noises, beating the ground with their paws or even making short charges. They may start growling, and their ears lie flat to their heads. Some bears do attack humans for food, but this is extremely rare – and they don't give any warning signs first. Running away from a bear just encourages them to start chasing.

193 Many grizzlies have learnt that they will find a free lunch wherever there are people. If grizzlies overcome their fear of humans they can become very dangerous. Once they have found a place where they can get food, they will return to it again and again.

◀ Being 'bear aware' can be a life-saver in some parts of the world. Bears are most dangerous when startled, so making plenty of noise when you're hiking in bear territory is one way of preventing an attack.

194

Dogs are being used in the Canadian Rocky Mountains to help train grizzlies to stay away from humans. Troublesome bears that wander close to areas where there are lots of people are sedated with drugs that send them to sleep. When they wake up, the dogs bark and growl at them, chasing them away until they reach the safety of the woodlands. The bears quickly learn to stay away from houses!

195

American black bears are often feared by campers, but they rarely attack people. In fact bears have much more reason to fear humans than we have to fear them. Around 30 to 40 people have been killed by black bears in the United States in the last 100 years, but 30,000 of these beautiful creatures are killed by humans every year.

Bear scare!

The advice if you see a bear up close is to slowly back away, watching it all the time. If the bear follows you, stand and wave your arms around while shouting loudly. The idea is to frighten the bear away, so you have to look as mean and angry as you can! Practise your angry face and shouting — you'll probably find it quite easy!

▶ A bear that was trapped near a town and examined by scientists as part of a study is chased away by a specially trained dog. This will keep it from returning to the area.

Harm and help

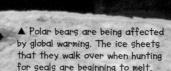

▲ Polar bears are being affected by global warming. The ice sheets that they walk over when hunting for seals are beginning to melt.

196 **Bears are being forced to live in smaller and smaller areas.** Of the eight types of bear, all are threatened with extinction, except brown bears and American black bears.

197 Bears are killed when people believe them to be a danger, or when they eat crops. They are also taken from the wild to be sold as pets, or to be used in traditional medicine. Wildlife organizations are involved in fighting against illegal trade in bear parts.

198 **Most bears are suffering because their habitats (where they live) are being taken away from them.** People have turned forests and woodlands into farms, mines, towns and cities. Even polar bears are in decline, because their habitat is affected by global warming. Loss of habitat is the greatest threat to bear survival.

QUIZ

1. What is the name of the only South American bear?
2. What is the other name for an Asiatic black bear?
3. Where would you find giant pandas?
4. Where do polar bears live, the South Pole or the North Pole?

Answers:
1. Spectacled bear 2. Moon bear
3. China 4. North Pole

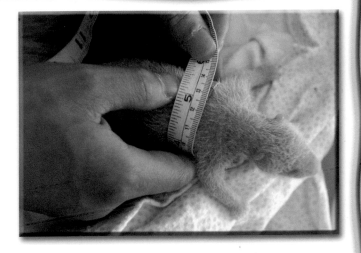

▶ A tiny panda cub is measured at the China conservation and research centre for the giant panda.

199 There are about 50 panda reserves in China, where most of the nation's giant pandas are protected. Despite this, many are still killed or captured by poachers every year. Groups of pandas are also split up, living in small areas of forest, separated from one another. This makes it difficult for pandas to meet up and breed successfully.

▼ Spectacled bears are categorized as 'vulnerable'. This means the species is already under threat and help is urgently needed over the coming years.

200 As humans take over more and more of the natural world for their own use, animals and plants are being wiped off the planet. People today face a tough challenge — will they work hard to save bears, or push them further towards extinction?

Hunters of the sky

201 Birds of prey are magnificent hunters of the sky. They soar through the air using their large wings to keep them aloft, as they scan the ground below for food. Some birds of prey, such as eagles, are hunters and kill to eat. Others, such as vultures, eat carrion (dead animals). Birds of prey are also called raptors, from the Latin *rapere*, meaning to grab or seize, because they kill with their feet.

▼ A long-legged buzzard brings food to its chicks. These birds of prey nest on cliff ledges and feed on small mammals, reptiles and large insects.

Eagle-eyed predators

202 Like all hunters, birds of prey need to be kitted out with tools. They have sharp senses, muscular bodies, tough beaks and grasping feet with sharp talons. They can detect prey from great distances and launch deadly attacks with skill and accuracy. Some can fly at super speeds.

▼ Golden eagles are large birds, measuring about 2 metres from wing tip to wing tip.

Finger-like primary flight feathers at wing tips

Rusty brown feathers

203 Raptors are able to fly high above the ground. The sky not only offers a great view of prey, it is also a safe place for birds as they search. As adults, birds of prey do have natural enemies, but even on land they are usually a match for most other predators due to their size.

204 Good eyesight is essential for raptors. They need to be able to locate prey that is in grass or under cover, often from a great distance. Birds of prey have eyes that are packed with light-detecting cells. The eyes are positioned near the front of the head, which means a bird can see well in front, to the side and partly around to the back.

▼ Birds of prey have large eyes that face forwards, to give them excellent vision.

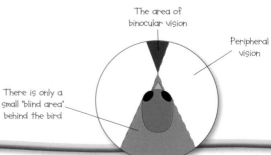

The area of binocular vision

Peripheral vision

There is only a small 'blind area' behind the bird

QUIZ
Which of these animals are predators and which are prey?
Leopard Warthog
Eagle Crocodile
Tortoise Wildebeest

Answers:
Predators: leopard, eagle, crocodile
Prey: warthog, tortoise, wildebeest

205 Birds of prey have big, powerful bodies. This helps them catch and kill food, but means they need more energy to fly. Meat is an energy-packed food, ideal for building muscles. Even the largest birds of prey can swoop and soar, although smaller birds are usually more acrobatic in flight.

Pale feathers on crown

Large bill

Large, broad wings

White-tailed eagle
Large, heavy bill

▶ Eagles and vultures have big, tough bills, but falcons have smaller, sharp bills. A bird's bill and talons are made of a hard substance called keratin, the same as our nails.

Large tail

Egyptian vulture
Long, hooked bill

Powerful feet with sharp talons

Birds of prey may carry their food to a safe place to eat it, but others eat their prey where it was killed

206 Scientists used to think that all birds of prey had a poor sense of smell. The turkey vulture is the only bird of prey known to have a good sense of smell, and probably the only one able to smell out its food. They can detect carrion on the ground while they are flying.

Gyrfalcon
Short bill with a sharp hook

Where in the world?

▲ Steller's sea eagle eats mainly fish, so this bird of prey lives near rivers, lakes and seashores. It only breeds in far eastern Russia.

207 **Warm, tropical regions are home to many species (types) of birds of prey.** They live on grasslands or in rainforests where there is lots to eat. Away from the tropics there are fewer raptors. Their habitats include forests, wetlands and coastal areas.

▼ Peregrine falcons are one of the world's most common birds of prey and they live on every continent, except Antarctica.

208 **Birds of prey live all over the world, except Antarctica.** No raptors can survive the freezing conditions of the south polar region, where food is scarce. Some are able to find food and endure the cold of the northern Arctic area. Snowy owls, peregrine falcons and white-tailed eagles can all cope with the cold, but travel to warmer places when the worst weather bites.

▶ Vultures and a jackal fight over the carcass of a zebra on an African grassland.

209 Some birds of prey can live in different habitats in different parts of the world. Ospreys and peregrine falcons are found in the Americas, Africa, Asia, Europe and Australia. Ospreys prefer to live near water, while peregrines like hills, cliffs and even cities.

▶ This family of Harris hawks has made a prickly home out of a cactus. In deserts, trees are scarce.

210 Barn owls live in many parts of the world, but one of their favourite places to build a nest is inside an old building. They frequently choose barns or church steeples to live in, where they are unlikely to be disturbed and can find a good supply of small rodents to eat.

211 Harris hawks hunt in deserts and other dry places. Small animals that live in these places often stay hidden from view and out of the strong sunlight, which makes them hard to find. Smart Harris hawks deal with this problem by living and hunting in groups, which makes it easier for them to seek and kill their fast-moving prey.

Little and large

212 **The largest birds of prey are Andean condors.** Their wingspan, which is measured from wing tip to wing tip, can be 3 metres in males. Condors have the biggest wings of all birds, which can catch the wind to soar above mountains at incredible heights of 5.5 kilometres.

Andean condor
Body length: 120 centimetres
Average wingspan: 3 metres

▶ These wings are shown to scale. Large birds with big wings are able to soar and travel long distances. Birds with smaller wings are more agile in flight and can hunt at greater speeds.

Black-thighed falconet

213 **In Europe, the largest raptors are white-tailed eagles.** They are found from Greenland to Turkey, but there are just 10,000 in the wild. These birds came close to extinction after years of shooting and poisoning, but are now protected in many countries. In Australia, the largest raptors are wedge-tailed eagles. They can grow to more than one metre long, with a wingspan of up to 2.3 metres.

◀ Little black-thighed falconets can easily dart through forests to hunt prey because of their small size.

214 **The smallest birds of prey are the falconets from Southeast Asia.** There are five species and the smallest are the white-fronted falconet and the black-thighed falconet. Falconets are just 14 to 18 centimetres long from bill to tail tip. Most feed on insects, but the pied falconet, which is the largest, can catch small animals.

MEASURING SIZE

Using a measuring tape, discover just how large or small these birds are. If you were standing next to an Eurasian eagle owl, would it reach your waist? If your arms were wings, what would your wingspan measure?

Eurasian eagle owl
Body length: 70 centimetres
Average wingspan: 2 metres

215 Some owls
are big birds. Eurasian eagle
owls are about 70 centimetres tall
and they are large enough to hunt deer
fawns, although they also eat beetles, rats
and voles. They can hunt in forests, but they
prefer open spaces.

Common buzzard
Body length: 48 centimetres
Average wingspan: 125 centimetres

216 The largest bird of prey that ever
lived was probably Haast's eagle. It lived in New
Zealand until around 500 years ago. Six million years
ago, a giant bird called *Argentavis* flew across
what is now Argentina. It had a body
like a condor, but its wingspan was
similar to that of a small plane!

Black-thighed falconet
Body length: 15 centimetres
Average wingspan:
30 centimetres

Hovering and soaring

217 Birds of prey have one advantage over most other predators – they can fly. Flying allows creatures to escape from other animals and stay safe. They can explore new areas easily as they search for food, mates or places to breed.

218 Birds' bodies are perfectly adapted for flying. They have light bones that are mostly hollow, but still strong. Their big hearts and lungs can collect lots of oxygen with every breath. This is the gas that animals need to turn their food into energy.

Narrow, pointed wings

Metacarpals – form a 'hand'

Wingbeats are stiff and shallow

Skull

Humerus – similar to our upper arm bone

Keel – where large flight muscles are attached

Ribs

▶ Hovering and flying require lots of energy, so kestrels have light bodies with muscles and powerful wings. Their skeleton is very light and flexible, but also strong and rigid.

The long tail feathers are spread out to keep the bird steady while it is hovering, looking for food

I DON'T BELIEVE IT!

Hobbies are amongst the fastest, most acrobatic fliers of all. They can dive, twist and turn, bombing towards the ground at great speeds, only opening their wings a few metres above the ground.

219 Kestrels hover and look as if they are hardly moving. They fly facing the wind, staying in the same spot above the ground. Kestrels spread their tails and the feathers at their wing tips turn up, which helps them to stay steady. As they lower their heads, they get a good view of the ground and any small animals, before launching an attack.

220

Birds of prey with long, broad wings soar through the sky. They also have large, fan-shaped tails that, with their wings, catch the air like a parachute. Soaring birds, such as eagles and vultures, often wait until the air is warm before they fly. As air is heated by the Sun it rises. Large, soaring birds use these flows of warm air, called thermal uplifts, to get airborne and rise high above the ground.

As ground air is heated, it becomes lighter

Lighter, warmer air rises, creating thermals

Thermals help big birds fly high and soar

▲ Thermals are hot air currents that travel upwards. Birds of prey use them to reach greater heights.

221

At breeding time, male birds of prey often perform display flights. These might help to attract females or mark out territory. There are different patterns of display flights, from circling round and round, to dive bombing or swooping up and down.

▶ At mating time, one golden eagle dives towards its mate, which turns its back, and they wrestle one another with their feet.

101

Nests, eggs and chicks

222 Like all birds, raptors lay eggs, usually in nests. Females may build nests in trees or on cliffs. Some birds of prey use the same nest every year, adding more sticks until it is huge. Golden eagle nests can eventually grow to 6 metres deep and 2 metres wide!

▶ Ospreys often use the same nest, year after year, so their nest becomes massive.

223 Big birds of prey have few natural predators, so only lay one or two eggs a year. Caring for chicks is hard work because they need a lot of food. If large birds of prey had more chicks, they might not be able to find enough food to feed them all and some would die. Smaller birds of prey usually breed earlier in the year and lay more eggs.

224 One egg is laid at a time and the female sits on it to keep it warm. It can take several days before all the eggs are laid. While the female protects the eggs and chicks, the male does most of the hunting and brings food to the nest. When the chicks hatch, they are covered in soft feathers called down.

QUIZ
The nest of a bird of prey, especially an eagle, is called an eyrie. Match these animals to their homes:
Den   Spider
Hive   Rabbit
Burrow Bee
Web   Bear

Answers:
Den/Bear, Hive/Bee,
Burrow/Rabbit, Web/Spider

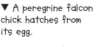

▼ A peregrine falcon chick hatches from its egg.

▶ At two days old, the chick is fluffy and cheeps for food.

225 If food is scarce, the smallest chicks are not fed and die. Eagle chicks battle with each other and a larger, hungrier chick may push its brother or sister out of the nest or even eat it. It takes just a few weeks for the chicks of a small bird of prey, such as a merlin, to grow adult feathers and be able to fly, but it can take over four months for vulture chicks to reach this stage.

226 Young birds of prey may stay in their parents' care for many months. They have to learn how to hunt before they become independent, and might rely on their parents to bring them food for a whole year after hatching. When they are old enough to mate they may find a partner and stay with them for life.

▼ When it is 28 days old, the young bird is growing its adult plumage (feathers) and the old down is falling out.

▶ Juvenile peregrines have brown feathers. The face markings are paler than in older birds.

Home and away

227 **Birds of prey may fly long distances (migrate) in search of food or places to breed.** Raptors that live near the Equator don't usually migrate as their tropical homes contain enough food and are warm all year round.

▼ Migrating birds of prey follow certain routes every year. Some of the major migration routes are shown here.

Hawk Mountain

Veracruz

228 **Animals of the north struggle to survive in the cold.** Many small animals hibernate (sleep) during winter. This leaves some birds of prey hungry, so they travel south to warmer areas. Golden eagles, gyrfalcons and goshawks stay in their northerly homes unless they live in the extreme north.

▼ Every year, people gather to watch birds fly overhead at Hawk Mountain, USA.

229 **Migrating birds usually fly over land, not water.** Warm air currents that help large birds to soar for long distances develop above continents rather than oceans, so the routes avoid stretches of water. Big groups of birds may fly together over strips of land and crossing points, such as at Gibraltar, where Europe meets Africa, or the Black Sea coast.

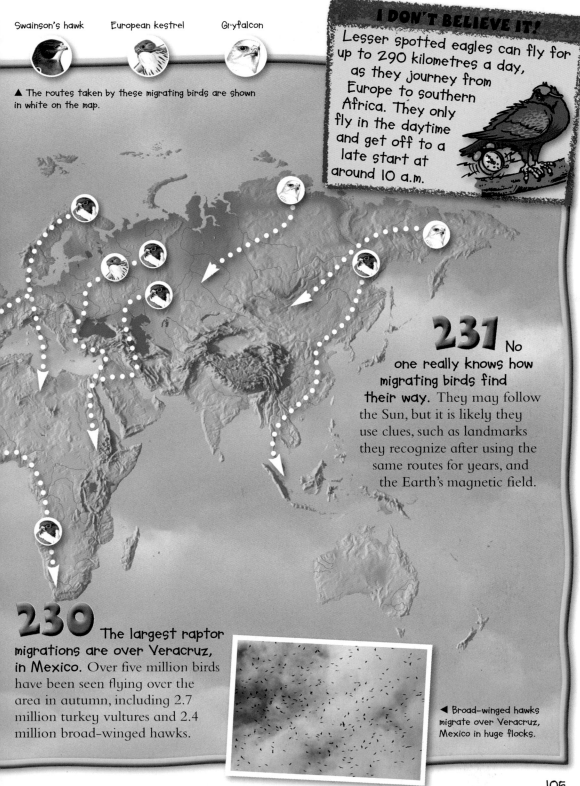

Swainson's hawk European kestrel Gyrfalcon

▲ The routes taken by these migrating birds are shown in white on the map.

231 No one really knows how migrating birds find their way. They may follow the Sun, but it is likely they use clues, such as landmarks they recognize after using the same routes for years, and the Earth's magnetic field.

230 The largest raptor migrations are over Veracruz, in Mexico. Over five million birds have been seen flying over the area in autumn, including 2.7 million turkey vultures and 2.4 million broad-winged hawks.

◀ Broad-winged hawks migrate over Veracruz, Mexico in huge flocks.

Hunting weapons

232 Predators need good senses to find prey, speed to catch it and weapons for killing it. Raptors are equipped with bodies that are ideal for locating and killing, but learning the skills to hunt takes time, patience and practice.

◄ Tawny owls have soft feathers that muffle noise, so they can take off in silence.

233 The most important weapons are feet and mouths. Raptors' bills are usually hooked, with a pointed tip. Birds that hunt other birds, such as falcons, hawks and owls, often have short, hooked bills. Those raptors that hunt larger animals need long, strong bills.

▼ This golden eagle's toes have dagger-like claws (talons) that can pierce flesh with ease.

234 Raptors' feet have talons and they are highly developed for hunting. Each foot has three strong, scaly toes at the front and one at the side or back. When the toes are bent they can grasp like a hand – perfect for holding wriggling prey.

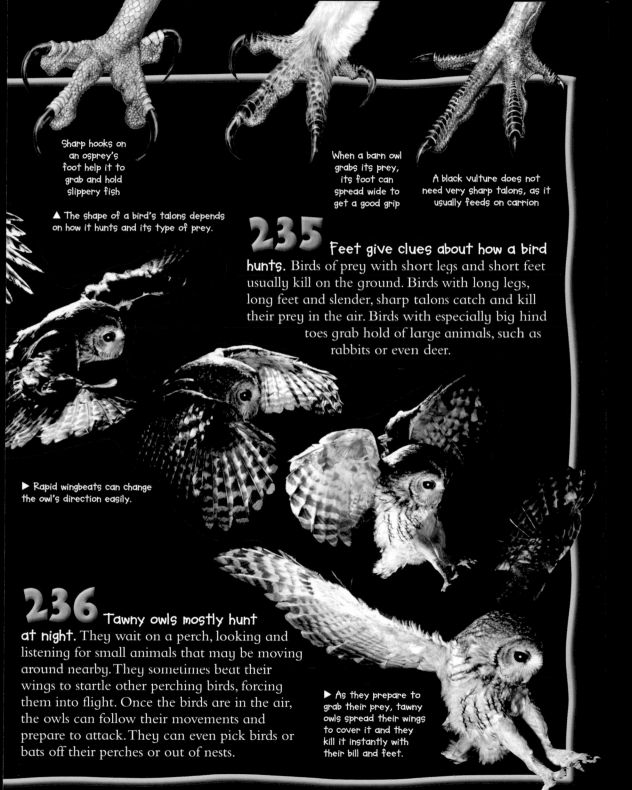

Sharp hooks on an osprey's foot help it to grab and hold slippery fish

When a barn owl grabs its prey, its foot can spread wide to get a good grip

A black vulture does not need very sharp talons, as it usually feeds on carrion

▲ The shape of a bird's talons depends on how it hunts and its type of prey.

235 Feet give clues about how a bird hunts. Birds of prey with short legs and short feet usually kill on the ground. Birds with long legs, long feet and slender, sharp talons catch and kill their prey in the air. Birds with especially big hind toes grab hold of large animals, such as rabbits or even deer.

▶ Rapid wingbeats can change the owl's direction easily.

236 Tawny owls mostly hunt at night. They wait on a perch, looking and listening for small animals that may be moving around nearby. They sometimes beat their wings to startle other perching birds, forcing them into flight. Once the birds are in the air, the owls can follow their movements and prepare to attack. They can even pick birds or bats off their perches or out of nests.

▶ As they prepare to grab their prey, tawny owls spread their wings to cover it and they kill it instantly with their bill and feet.

Scrounging scavengers

◀ Vultures and marabou storks feast on the carcass of a dead animal.

237 **Not all birds of prey hunt live prey.** Some eat any meat they can find and are called scavengers, or carrion-eaters. Some birds of prey only scavenge when they cannot find live prey, but others never hunt and only eat leftovers.

238 Vultures are birds of prey that mostly scavenge dead animals. They often have bald heads and necks because feathers would get messy and bloody from delving into dead bodies. Vultures often look for hyenas or lions tucking into a meal, then swoop down to feed when the coast is clear.

King vulture

Lammergeier

Lappet-faced vulture

▶ Adult griffon vultures have white feathers on their necks, a yellow–white bill and yellow-brown eyes. Youngsters have darker feathers, brown bills and eyes.

239
Griffon vultures like to wash in water after feeding. They have bare heads and necks for reaching into carcasses. These birds soar over open areas, using their long, broad wings, looking for carrion. Griffon vultures fly in groups of up to 40 for hours at a time and they may frighten other predators away to get at food.

241
African vultures take turns to munch through a body. Lappet-faced vultures have big bills that are perfect for ripping through skin and fur, so they often eat first. Hooded vultures come along later to eat softer meat, and lammergeiers (bearded vultures) tackle the leftovers.

◀ Few animals are clever enough to use tools, but Egyptian vultures can break tough eggs with stones.

240
Vultures and other scavenging birds make the most of any dining opportunities. Turkey vultures are often seen flying or perched near roads – ready to tuck in when animals and cars collide on the highway. Egyptian vultures find it difficult to break open eggs with their bill, so they use stones to crack them open instead.

◀ Vultures usually have long, thin necks that help them probe deep into a carcass to feed. Their bills are particularly long and strong, because carrion is tough to eat.

Fussy eaters

242 **Some birds of prey have unusual diets.** Lesser spotted eagles that live around wetlands feast on frogs. Snail kites have curved, hooked bills for extracting snails from their shells. Palm-nut vultures eat the fruits of palm trees.

▲ When ospreys plunge into water, they close their nostrils so the water doesn't shoot up into their nose. They carry their catch back to the nest to eat in peace or feed it to their chicks.

▶ Snail kites live in South American wetlands and eat water snails, turtles and crabs. They also hunt rodents, such as rats and mice.

243 **Plucking a fish out of water takes huge skill.** Yet some birds of prey can achieve this incredible feat. They soar over water, watching for movement at the surface. Once they have spied a fish, the birds dive down and plunge their feet into the water to grab it. This requires sharp eyesight, quick reactions and an agile body.

244 **Ospreys are fish-eaters.** These birds of prey nest near lakes and rivers or by clean, calm coastal areas. They hover up to 30 metres above the water until they spot a fish. Then they dive down with half-closed wings and stretch out their legs and feet just before hitting the water.

245

White-tailed eagles pluck both fish and ducks out of the water. They perch on trees and swoop down to grab prey. Sharp growths, called spicules, on the feet help to grip wet prey and large bills are ideal for ripping and tearing flesh.

246

Lammergeiers eat a diet of bones and scraps left behind by other predators. They pick up large bones with their feet and fly to a height of 80 metres before dropping the bones to the ground to split them. These birds also drop tortoises to get to the soft flesh inside the shell.

FISH EATERS

Penguins are flightless birds that catch fish to eat. Find out where they live and how they catch fish. How are their bodies different to those of birds of prey?

▶ If a bone is dropped from a great height it splits open. The lammergeier can then eat the soft marrow inside.

Snake stampers

Black flight feathers

Black crest feathers

247 Secretary birds are not like other raptors. They are tall, elegant and long-legged. These birds stride through the long grasses of African plains, looking for insects and other animals to eat. When they find their prey, they stamp and peck it to death.

Grey plumage on body

248 Secretary birds eat snakes, even poisonous ones, such as cobras and adders. When it spies a snake in the vegetation, a secretary bird runs towards it and stamps on it, or inflicts a kick to the head. A sharp peck to the back of the snake's neck finishes it off. If the prey proves too tough to kill this way, the bird may grab it in its beak, take to the skies and drop it from a great height.

Large feet

Long legs

▶ A male secretary bird can grow to about 1.4 metres tall. Secretary birds might get their name from the crest of long, black quill feathers on their heads, which look like old-fashioned ink pens.

249
Snakes are no match for a secretary bird. These predators run fast during a chase and their legs are covered in thick scales to protect them from bites. If a snake fights back, the secretary bird spreads its wings to form a shield. The flapping wings scare the snake and if it bites a feather, the bird will suffer no harm. They often hunt in pairs and can walk more than 25 kilometres every day in search of food.

QUIZ
1. How tall can a male secretary bird grow to be?
2. What are secretary birds' legs covered in?
3. How many snakes does a family of short-toed eagles need every day?

Answers:
1. About 1.4 metres
2. Thick scales 3. At least five

250
When they are angry, excited or scared, secretary birds raise their quill feathers. Their body feathers are grey and white, but black feathers at the top of their long legs make them appear as if they are wearing short trousers! Males and females look similar, but females are smaller.

▶ Short-toed eagles feed dead snakes to their young, which have enormous appetites.

251
Not many birds of prey eat snakes, but short-toed eagles eat almost nothing else. They attack snakes that are nearly 2 metres long and even eat poisonous ones. A family of short-toed eagles needs at least five snakes every day, so the adults spend a lot of time hunting their slithery prey.

113

Eagles

252 Eagles are large, heavy-bodied birds with strong legs, big bills and feet, and broad wings. They are usually smaller than vultures, but larger than most other birds of prey. There are about 60 types, including fish eagles, snake eagles, harpy eagles and hawk eagles.

253 These birds live in all regions of the world except Antarctica. Golden eagles are one of the most common, widespread types. There may be as many as one million and they live in North America, Europe and Asia, around mountains, forests and cliffs. The Great Nicobar serpent eagle is a rare eagle. It lives on one small island near India, and there may be fewer than 1000.

254 Eagles are not as agile as some other birds of prey. When they hunt, they are more likely to soar and stoop than to hover and dive. Eagles often perch to watch for prey, then swoop in low for the kill.

▼ Large birds of prey, such as eagles, rely on thermals to reach height in the sky.

2 An eagle uses thermals to reach a good height for spotting its prey, and then swoops.

1 Warm air thermals travel upwards.

4 The eagle flies off with its prey held firmly in its feet.

3 As the bird flies towards its prey, it swings its feet forward to grab hold of it.

255

The lowland forests of South America are home to the impressive-looking harpy eagle. These birds of prey are huge and can grow to over one metre long, with wingspans of 2 metres. They have large, two-pointed crests on their heads and their massive feet are the size of a grizzly bear's paw. Harpy eagles hunt tree-dwelling animals, such as monkeys and sloths, which they chase through the branches.

▲ Male harpy eagles have grey feathers on their heads and black plumage on their chests and backs. Females are paler.

256

Bald eagles are the national emblem of the USA. They have white heads and tails and yellow bills, which makes them easy to identify. Youngsters have brown feathers and do not develop their white markings until they are four or five years old. Bald eagles will eat almost anything, from carrion to fish, which they might steal from other birds.

I DON'T BELIEVE IT!

Harpy eagles may be named after winged creatures called harpies, from Greek mythology. Harpies had a woman's face and a vulture's body or were winged spirits that snatched food.

▶ Male and female bald eagles are almost identical in appearance, although females are usually slightly bigger than their mates.

Kites and buzzards

257 Kites are small raptors with short bills and long, narrow wings and tails. They are elegant fliers that flap their wings slowly. Kites catch small prey, such as insects and rodents. They live throughout the world, mostly in warm places.

◀ Swallow-tailed kites rarely flap their wings while flying, but twist their tails to change direction quickly.

258 Black kites are omnivores, which means they will eat almost anything. They even scavenge rubbish. These birds live in Africa, Australia, Europe and parts of Asia, especially in woods, near farmland and water, or where humans are found. Red kites are rarer and only found in parts of Europe. They mostly eat other birds, but will also eat whatever is available.

▶ Red kites hunt over grasslands, lakes and rubbish dumps. They also search roads for roadkill.

259 Swallow-tailed kites live in tropical rainforests of South America. They have long, elegant wings and forked tails that give them the appearance of swallows. These birds can swoop, soar and dive, changing direction rapidly to pursue prey. They build their nests at the tops of tall trees.

260 Buzzards are big-bodied birds with broad wings and large, rounded tails. When they fly, they beat their wings slowly and gracefully. They eat small mammals and insects. Honey buzzards eat wasps and bees. They rip open hives with their talons and bills, then eat the larvae, pupae and adult insects. These birds have slit-like nostrils and bristles instead of feathers between their eyes, which may protect them from stings.

261 In the Americas, buzzards are often called hawks. Swainson's hawk spends summer in the USA and travels to South America for winter. When breeding, they eat mice, squirrels and reptiles, but for the rest of the year they survive mostly on insects, such as grasshoppers and beetles. They often walk along the ground looking for food and sometimes hunt in teams.

◄ A common buzzard feeds during winter. There are nearly 30 species (types) of buzzards and they belong to a group of raptors called Buteos.

QUIZ

1. Which kites have the appearance of swallows?
2. Which buzzards eat wasps and bees?
3. Which hawk sometimes hunts in teams?

Answers:
1. Swallow-tailed kites
2. Honey buzzards
3. Swainson's hawk

117

Fast falcons

▶ A peregrine falcon pursues a swallow. It has recently been discovered that peregrines that live in towns are able to hunt at night, helped by city lights to find their prey.

262 **A peregrine falcon can move faster than any other animal on Earth.** These birds reach speeds of 100 kilometres an hour when chasing prey. When peregrines stoop from heights of one kilometre and plummet through the sky, they may reach speeds of 300 kilometres an hour or more.

263 Peregrines are travellers and have one of the longest migrations of any raptors. American peregrines have been known to cover 25,000 kilometres in just one year. These raptors are the most widespread of all birds of prey and live on every continent except Antarctica, but they are rare.

▼ Saker falcons have bold markings while some Eleonora's falcons have rusty pink breast feathers.

Eleonora's falcon

Saker falcon

264 There are about 35 species of falcon and most of them are speedy fliers. They are medium-sized raptors with muscle-packed bodies, pointed wings and short tails. They usually nest in cliffs and lay several eggs at a time. Falcons prey upon birds and other small animals.

▶ Gyrfalcons are bulky birds with extra body fat that helps them to keep warm.

265 Gyrfalcons can cope with the cold and they live around the Earth's frozen north. Some gyrfalcons are brown or grey. The further north they live, the paler they become, so they are camouflaged against the snowy landscape. These are the biggest falcons, with a wingspan of up to 1.3 metres, so they can pursue large prey such as ptarmigans, gulls and geese.

▼ Lesser kestrels spend the winters in Africa, travelling into Europe for the summer. They mostly feed on insects, but in spring they hunt reptiles and small mammals.

266 Kestrels are types of falcon that hover before attacking their prey. These small birds of prey have rounded heads and large eyes. While male and female raptors often have the same colour plumage, male kestrels are usually more colourful than the females.

Hawks and harriers

▼ Goshawks live in forested areas of Europe. They mainly hunt birds that are weak or ill because sick animals make easier targets.

267 Hawks, sparrowhawks and goshawks belong to a group of raptors called Accipiters. They are medium-sized birds and live in forests and woodlands. Short, rounded wings and long tails help them to fly in short bursts between trees, darting through branches in pursuit of small mammals and birds.

268 Most hawks hunt rodents, such as rats. They are useful because they eat pests that damage crops. However goshawks hunt game birds and poultry. Game birds, such as pheasants, are bred by farmers to be hunted for sport. Poultry, such as chickens, are an important food for humans. Goshawks have been killed to stop them from hunting these birds.

I DON'T BELIEVE IT!
Sharp-shinned hawks of America take their prey to a special perch called a butcher's block. This is where the raptor plucks all the feathers or fur off its prey, so these bits don't mess up its nest!

270 Harriers are raptors that look similar to hawks, with long legs and tails. They often fly low over fields and meadows, scouring the ground for snakes, frogs, insects, small birds or mammals. Hen harriers live in Europe, Asia and North America, but the populations of birds on each side of the Atlantic are slightly different from one another. North American birds are usually called marsh harriers or northern harriers.

269 Hawks may squeeze their prey to death. Many raptors use their feet to hold prey and their bills to kill it. Cooper's hawks hold a captured animal with their sharp talons and fly with it until it dies. They have been known to hold prey underwater to drown it.

Common black hawks live near water in Central America

▶ Hawks have rounded heads with short bills. Their compact bodies help them to fly fast and change direction.

Red-tailed hawks of North America inhabit woods, deserts and mountains

271 Eurasian sparrowhawks are one of the most common raptors in the world. They live in forests, farms, woods and parks across Europe and Asia during the spring and summer, and travel south for the winter. Despite being common, sparrowhawks are so secretive that they are rarely seen. However when food is scarce they may investigate gardens, searching for song birds such as sparrows to eat.

Eurasian sparrowhawks hide their nests in woodlands

Hunters of the night

272 **Most owls hunt at night.** As well as having talons and sharp bills, owls have big eyes that face the front and can see depth and movement. Eyes have two types of cells – one detecting colours, the other just faint or dim light. Some owls only have light-detecting cells and can see in the darkness, but not colour.

273 **Owls use feathers to help them hear and to stop animals from hearing them.** Their ears are covered by feathers that direct sound into the ear canal. Downy feathers on the body and feet help to soften sound as the bird moves. Feathers on the wings are arranged in a way that deadens the sound of flapping, so the bird descends silently on its prey.

▲ Like some other owls, this great horned owl is nocturnal, which means that it is most active at night. It begins hunting at dusk and settles down to sleep when the Sun rises.

◄ Owls have three eyelids. The third eyelid is a special membrane that sweeps over the eye to clean it.

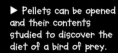

▶ Pellets can be opened and their contents studied to discover the diet of a bird of prey.

Pellet from a little owl

Pellet from a long-eared owl

Pellet from a barn owl

Pellet from a red kite

276 Owls eat a range of food, including insects, birds, bats and fish, and they often swallow an animal whole. Like other birds of prey, owls are not able to digest the hard parts of a body, such as bones, fur or feathers. They bring them up from their stomach and spit them out in the form of pellets. It takes about seven hours for one pellet to form.

274 Eurasian eagle owls have a wingspan of nearly 2 metres. The largest owls, they attack other birds to steal their territories. Tiny elf owls catch their prey in flight. They are the smallest owls, with a wingspan of just 15 centimetres.

275 Many birds of prey build their own nests, but owls do not. They either use old nests left by other birds, or they lay their eggs in a hole in a tree, a hollow in the ground or inside an abandoned building. Owls usually lay a clutch of up to seven eggs at a time and the chicks are called owlets.

▶ Tawny owls nest in tree hollows. They lay 2–6 eggs and the fluffy chicks do not leave the nest until they are about 35 days old.

Working birds

277 **Birds of prey can be trained to work with people.** This is called falconry or hawking, and is an old skill that has been around for about 2500 years. The first trained birds of prey were probably used to catch birds for people to eat. In some places it is against the law to catch wild birds for use in falconry, so birds are specially bred.

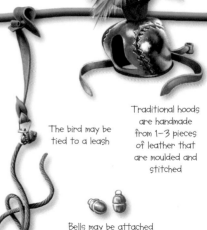

Traditional hoods are handmade from 1–3 pieces of leather that are moulded and stitched

The bird may be tied to a leash

Bells may be attached to anklets on the bird's legs or fitted to the tail

A falconer pulls the hood off using the top knot

▼ ▶ Falconers use a range of equipment to train and fly their birds, such as this peregrine falcon.

A swing lure is used to train a falcon and is made from the wing of another bird

Hood braces are gently pulled to tighten the hood on the bird's head

278 **Birds most commonly trained are Harris hawks, peregrine falcons, sparrowhawks and goshawks, because they are intelligent.** Training takes time and patience. The first step is to get the bird used to people. Next, it has to be trained to hop onto the falconer's gloved fist, then to fly away – and return. To start, the bird may be tied to a line, but as it learns to return, it is released. When the bird does what the falconer wants, it is rewarded with food.

SEE THEM FLY

Visit a place where birds of prey are kept, so you can watch them fly. This could be a nature reserve, wildlife park or a place where trained birds of prey display their skills.

279

Working raptors have been used to keep public places clear of pigeons. Pigeon poo can cause damage to buildings and spread diseases, so falconers and their birds visit city centres to stop the pigeons from nesting nearby. One sight of a swooping, soaring raptor scares the pigeons into flying elsewhere.

280

Birds of prey help farmers to control pests. Fields of berry-producing plants attract birds such as starlings. A flock can quickly strip the trees or bushes, leaving the farmer with no crop. Rather than covering the plants with expensive netting or spraying with chemicals, farmers ask falconers and their raptors to scare the smaller birds away.

281

Falcons can patrol airports to keep flocks of birds away from planes. If birds fly into a plane's engines, they can cause damage that is expensive to repair and can be dangerous. Airports sometimes play bird of prey calls to scare away flocks.

▶ Falcons have proved effective at keeping the skies clear of smaller birds at airports.

Bird tales

282 Throughout history, people have recognized the might and power of birds of prey and told stories about them. Native American legends tell of thunderbirds, which are large birds that create storms by flapping their wings. They also tell of an evil creature called Eagleman, which had the head of a man but the body and wings of an eagle.

▲ Native American wood carvings often showed thunderbirds with their huge bills and eyes.

▲ This ancient Greek coin is decorated with an owl.

283 Unlucky Prometheus was a character in Greek mythology. He stole fire from Zeus, the father of the gods, and gave it to mankind. This angered Zeus so much that he chained Prometheus to a rock and ordered that an eagle would eat his liver every day. By night, his liver grew back so Prometheus was destined to an eternity of pain and misery.

284 In ancient Egypt, Horus was a falcon god, worshipped as the god of the sky. According to legend, Horus's right eye was the sun and his left eye was the moon and, as he flew across the sky, the sun and moon moved with him. More than 2000 years ago, Horus' worshippers built the huge Temple of Edfu to honour him and it still stands in Egypt today, along the banks of the river Nile.

◀ Pictures of the falcon god Horus cover walls of ancient Egyptian temples and shrines.

I DON'T BELIEVE IT!

In ancient times, a Greek poet died after an eagle dropped a tortoise on his head. The raptor was probably trying to break the tortoise's shell and mistook the man's bald head for a large stone.

185 **A story from Finland tells how an eagle created the Earth and the heavens.** A woman called Luonnotar was floating in a giant ocean when an eagle made a nest on her knee and laid its eggs. However the nest fell, breaking the eggs. The shells became the heavens and Earth, the yolks became the sun and the egg whites became the moon.

▶ Griffins represented godly power and were often used to guard treasure, or to protect from evil.

186 **Griffins have featured in mythology and legends from Asia to Europe.** These fabled creatures were usually shown as lions with the heads of birds of prey, especially eagles.

Watching and tracking

287 Birdwatchers are called birders, while people who study birds more scientifically are called ornithologists. They use hides to watch raptors without disturbing them. Hides are covered in natural materials, such as branches or grass, for camouflage.

▲ A bird is trapped using a hawk mist net. Data taken from the bird will help to follow its movements and how it has grown.

288 Observing birds of prey is a fascinating hobby, but it is also an important job for scientists. They collect information to learn about how the birds live, where they migrate to and how many breeding adults there are. This work can then be used to follow how populations of birds of prey in different places increase or decrease.

289 Some birds of prey are studied using leg rings and by tracking their movements. They may be captured using a mist net, which catches birds in flight without harming them. Information is collected about each bird, such as its age, sex and size before an identity ring is put around its leg, or a tag is attached to its wing.

▼ Birds like these red kites can be studied from a hide. Birders use binoculars and telescopes to zoom in and watch them closely, without disturbing them.

ORDER FALCONIFORMES

Family	Number of species or types	Examples
Accipitridae	236	Kites, hawks, goshawks, buzzards, harriers, eagles, Old World vultures, sparrowhawks
Falconidae	64	Falcons, falconets, merlins, caracaras, kestrels
Cathartidae	7	New World vultures
Pandionidae	1	Osprey
Sagittariidae	1	Secretary bird

ORDER STRIGIFORMES

Family	Number of species or types	Examples
Tytonidae	21	Barn owls, bay owls and grass owls
Strigidae	159	Burrowing owl, eagle owl, fish owl, horned owls, long-eared owl, snowy owl, hawk owl

290 **Identifying birds of prey can be difficult.** Birders look for clues to help them work out what type of raptor they are observing, such as wing, tail and head shape. Colours and banding on plumage can also be used to discover what sex a bird is and whether it is a young bird or an adult. The way a raptor flies can also provide clues to identifying it.

▲ Owls are placed in the order Strigiformes. All other raptors are in a separate order, called Falconiformes.

MAKE A NOTE
When you see any bird you do not recognize make a note of its size, the shape of its wings and tail, the way it is behaving and the type of habitat you've seen it in. Use this information to discover its identity from a birdwatching book or website.

Raptors in peril

291 Birds of prey face few natural dangers, except those posed by humans and their way of life. Around half of all the world's species of migrating raptors are threatened with extinction. Many of these may die out because they are hunted or because their habitats are destroyed or polluted.

292 Raptors are killed by people who believe they are pests. Poison can be added to their food and left out for them to eat, or they may be shot. Birds and eggs are sometimes stolen from the wild by collectors or people who want to train birds for hawking or falconry.

▼ At night, barn owls may be confused by lights on roads or near towns and fly into the path of oncoming vehicles. Raptors can also be pulled into the sides of fast-moving lorries or cars.

Normal egg   Poisoned egg

▲ When female birds eat poisoned food, the poisons travel through their bodies and may reach the eggs growing inside them.

293
Habitats are damaged by chemicals used in farming or waste products from factories. When these chemicals enter birds' bodies – often by eating prey that have already been affected by them – they may cause permanent damage. Some chemicals stop eggshells from growing properly, so birds cannot produce healthy chicks.

295
Bateleurs live in open country across Africa, but their numbers are falling fast. They are struggling to survive because their natural habitat is being turned into farmland. Some large farming organizations are also poisoning them on purpose.

▶ Bateleur nests are disturbed as people settle near their habitats. Many birds are also trapped to be sold abroad.

▶ Long-billed vultures, such as this juvenile, are endangered.

294
When birds of prey drop in number, the environment suffers. Three species of Asian vultures help to stop the spread of disease to humans and other animals by eating carrion, but millions of these birds have died in just over ten years. The vultures are dying because a drug that is used to treat farm animals is deadly to any raptors that feed on their bodies.

Rescuing raptors

296 The Philippine eagle is one of the rarest raptors, but people are working hard to save it. There are probably fewer than 250 breeding pairs in the wild, although scientists have managed to breed them in captivity. The largest of all eagles, these birds have lost their homes to farmland and mines. Now they are protected by law and their land, nests and eggs are guarded.

▲ Even if the numbers of Philippine eagles stop falling, it may be impossible for the species to recover in the wild.

► Californian condors died in huge numbers after eating animals that had been shot with lead bullets. Lead is a poison that is still found in the environment.

298 Californian condors are vultures with wingspans of nearly 3 metres. They do not breed until they are about nine years old and only have one chick every two years. These birds once lived all over the USA, but by the 1980s there were very few left. They were all taken into captivity, making a total of 22. Since then they have been bred in protected places and some have been returned to the wild.

297 People who are interested in birds work together to protect them. BirdLife International is an organization that operates in more than 100 countries. It helps local conservation agencies protect birds' habitats and teach people how to respect the environment.

299 In many countries, endangered birds of prey are protected. It is illegal to hunt, trap or poison them. When protected raptors breed, nest locations are kept secret and volunteers may keep watch to make sure thieves do not steal the eggs. In some places, birds' habitats are protected and forests or woodlands cannot be turned into farmland or homes for people.

300 There are 24 types of raptor on the island of Madagascar and half of those are found nowhere else. People have campaigned to protect areas of habitat, such as the Manambolomaty Lakes, which are where the Madagascan fish eagle lives. Similar projects, called Species Survival Programs, have been set up in Madagascar and other places.

▲ Hand-rearing birds of prey is extremely difficult. Feeding them is more successful when the chick thinks a parent bird is looking after them.

▼ Birds that have been raised in captivity or treated for injuries or ill-health are always returned to the wild whenever possible. This bald eagle's release is a time of celebration for local bird-lovers.

Secretive serpents

301 Snakes have lived on our planet for more than 120 million years. There are nearly 3000 different species (type) of snake alive today. These spectacular, slithering serpents are superbly adapted to life without legs – the word 'serpent' means 'to creep'. Snakes are shy, secretive animals that avoid people whenever they can and will not usually attack unless they need to defend themselves.

▶ The first snakes to evolve were constricting snakes, such as this huge anaconda, which squeezes its prey to death in its strong coils.

What is a snake?

302 Snakes belong
to the animal family group
known as reptiles. They
are related to lizards,
turtles, tortoises, crocodiles
and alligators. Snakes
may have evolved from
swimming or burrowing
lizards that lived millions
of years ago, and are in
fact very distant cousins
of the dinosaurs!

303 Snakes have long,
thin bodies, with no legs,
eyelids or external (outside)
ears. They can't blink, so they
always seem to be staring. Some
lizards also have no legs, but they
do have eyelids and outer ears.

▼ More than three-quarters of snake
species, such as this python, aren't poisonous.

REPTILE FAMILY

Over half of all reptiles are
lizards – there are nearly
5000 species.

Amphisbaenians, or worm
lizards, are burrowing reptiles
that live underground.

Snakes are the
second largest
group of reptiles,
after lizards.
Hundreds of
species of snakes
are poisonous.

Tuataras are rare, ancient and
unusual reptiles from New Zealand.

Crocodiles, alligators,
gharials and caimans are
predators with long, narrow
snouts and sharp teeth.

Turtles and tortoises
have a hard shell on their
back, which protects them
from predators.

304 Like all reptiles,
snakes are covered in waterproof
scales. A snake's scales grow in the
top layers of its skin to protect its
body as it slides over the ground.
Scales allow skin to stretch when
the snake moves or feeds.

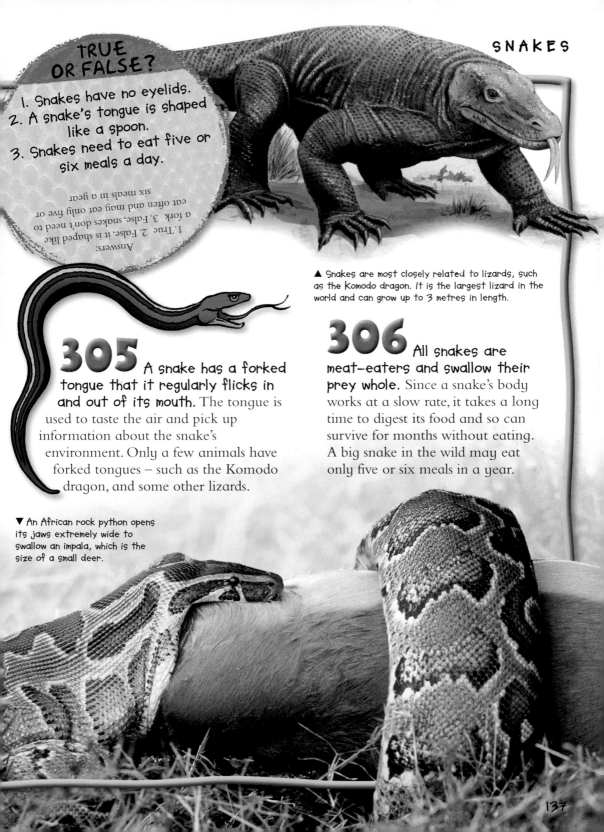

TRUE OR FALSE?

1. Snakes have no eyelids.
2. A snake's tongue is shaped like a spoon.
3. Snakes need to eat five or six meals a day.

Answers:
1. True 2. False, it is shaped like a fork 3. False, snakes don't need to eat often and may eat only five or six meals in a year.

▲ Snakes are most closely related to lizards, such as the Komodo dragon. It is the largest lizard in the world and can grow up to 3 metres in length.

305 A snake has a forked tongue that it regularly flicks in and out of its mouth. The tongue is used to taste the air and pick up information about the snake's environment. Only a few animals have forked tongues – such as the Komodo dragon, and some other lizards.

306 All snakes are meat-eaters and swallow their prey whole. Since a snake's body works at a slow rate, it takes a long time to digest its food and so can survive for months without eating. A big snake in the wild may eat only five or six meals in a year.

▼ An African rock python opens its jaws extremely wide to swallow an impala, which is the size of a small deer.

137

Where in the world?

307 Snakes live all over the world on almost every continent. There are no snakes on Antarctica, because it is too cold for them to survive. Snakes rely on their surroundings for warmth so they are most common in hot places, such as deserts and rainforests.

▶ This python lives in the rainforests of northeast Australia. Its waterproof skin helps to stop its body from drying out in the heat.

308 The greatest variety of snakes live in rainforest habitats. These warm places contain lots of food for snakes to eat and provide plenty of places to rest and shelter. Rainforests are always warm, enabling snakes to keep their body temperature up, which allows them to stay active all year round.

309 The most widespread snake in the world is the adder. This poisonous snake lives across Europe and Asia in a variety of habitats, including cold places. The adder's dark colour helps it to warm up quickly when it basks in sunlight, and it sleeps, or hibernates, through the cold winter months.

◀ Adders usually live in undisturbed countryside, from woodland and heathland to sand dunes and mountains.

▶ The sandy-coloured woma python is well camouflaged in its dry desert habitat (home).

310 In Australia there are more poisonous snakes than non-poisonous ones. Australia is home to the taipan snake, which has one of the strongest and most powerful poisons of any land snake. It is very secretive and lives in desert areas where there are very few people, so not many people get bitten.

Taipan

311 Sea snakes live in warm, tropical waters, such as the Indian and Pacific Oceans. Most sea snakes can take in oxygen from the water through their skin, but they have to come to the surface regularly to breathe air. When underwater, sea snakes close off their nostrils with special valves.

▶ Sea snakes have glands under their tongues that collect salt from their blood. When the snake flicks out its tongue the salt goes back into the water.

SNAKE HABITAT POSTER

You will need:
pen paper pictures of snakes
glue atlas

Using a pen and paper trace a world map from an atlas. Draw on the biggest mountains, forests and deserts and then draw or stick on pictures of snakes from wildlife magazines or the Internet.

Big and small

312 **The six biggest snakes are all boas and pythons.** They are the boa constrictor, the anaconda, the reticulated python, the Indian python, the African rock python and the scrub python. These snakes all take a long time to warm up and need to eat a lot to keep their massive bodies working.

313 **The longest snake in the world is the reticulated python.** An average adult can grow to around 6 metres in length, but it has been known to grow much longer. This snake has an effective camouflage pattern on its scaly skin to help hide its huge body, so it can lie in wait for its prey without being seen.

314 **The heaviest snake is the anaconda.** This enormous snake can be as thick as an adult human and weigh as much as five children! It lives in the rivers of the Amazon rainforest in South America, where the water helps to support its enormous bulk. An anaconda grows up to an impressive 7 or 8 metres long.

▼ It has taken nine people to support the weight of this 5-metre-long anaconda, from South America.

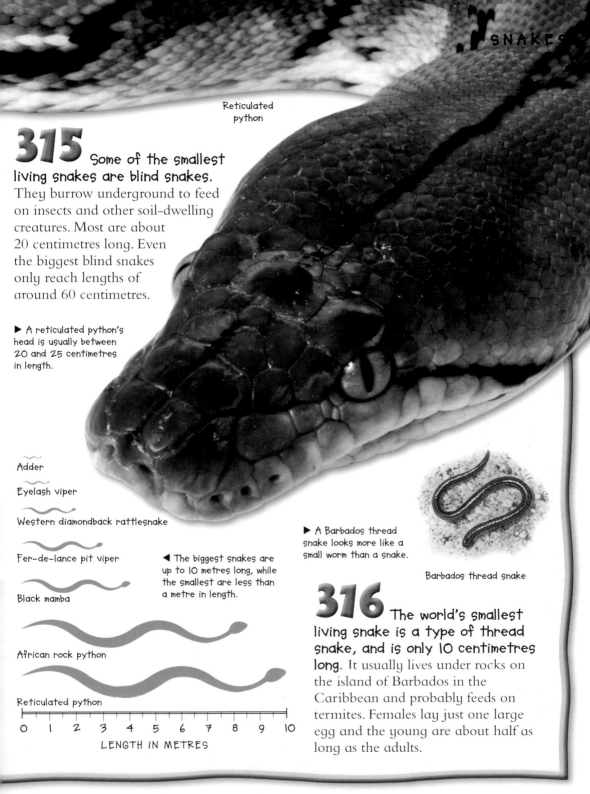

Reticulated python

315
Some of the smallest living snakes are blind snakes. They burrow underground to feed on insects and other soil-dwelling creatures. Most are about 20 centimetres long. Even the biggest blind snakes only reach lengths of around 60 centimetres.

▶ A reticulated python's head is usually between 20 and 25 centimetres in length.

Adder

Eyelash viper

Western diamondback rattlesnake

Fer-de-lance pit viper

◀ The biggest snakes are up to 10 metres long, while the smallest are less than a metre in length.

Black mamba

African rock python

Reticulated python

| 0 | 1 | 2 | 3 | 4 | 5 | 6 | 7 | 8 | 9 | 10 |

LENGTH IN METRES

▶ A Barbados thread snake looks more like a small worm than a snake.

Barbados thread snake

316
The world's smallest living snake is a type of thread snake, and is only 10 centimetres long. It usually lives under rocks on the island of Barbados in the Caribbean and probably feeds on termites. Females lay just one large egg and the young are about half as long as the adults.

Snake bodies

317 Snakes come in different shapes and sizes depending on their environment and lifestyle. They may be short, thick and slightly flattened, like a ground-dwelling rattlesnake, or long, thin and lightweight, like a tree snake. Burrowing snakes have tube-shaped bodies, which help them to slide through the soil.

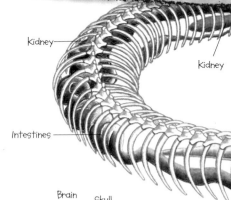

Kidney

Kidney

Intestines

Brain   Skull

Eye

Fangs

Tongue

Venom gland

Trachea (windpipe)

Triangular

Short, thick body

Loaf-shaped

Long, thin body

Tube-shaped body

▲ These cross sections show five different snake body shapes, with the backbone and a pair of ribs inside.

318 Some snakes, such as rattlesnakes, have a distinct head and neck region. Others, such as blind snakes, look much the same at both ends. Pythons and vipers have short tails, while the tails of some tree snakes are longer than their bodies.

◀ The Texas blind snake's eyes are two dark spots under three small scales across the top of its head.

▶ A rattlesnake has an arrow-shaped head because of the venom (poison) sacs behind its eyes.

319 There isn't much space inside a snake's body, so the organs are long and thin. Most snakes have only one working right lung, which does the work of two. A snake's skeleton consists mainly of a skull and a long, flexible backbone with up to 400 vertebrae (spine bones).

◄ The organs of this male water moccasin are elongated to fit into its long, thin body.

Tail

Rectum

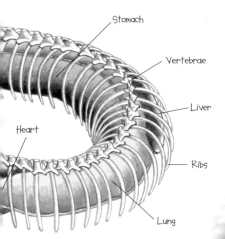

Stomach

Vertebrae

Liver

Heart

Ribs

Lung

320 Like all reptiles, snakes are cold-blooded. They can't keep their bodies at a constant temperature, the way warm-blooded mammals and birds do. Their bodies stay the same temperature as their surroundings, so they bask in the Sun, or on warm surfaces to gain heat, and move into shade, underground burrows or cool water to cool down.

▼ In cooler parts of North America, thousands of garter snakes often emerge together from their hibernation dens in spring.

321 In colder places, snakes often sleep through the long winter months, waking up in spring when the weather is warmer. This winter sleep is called hibernation. Snakes often hibernate in caves, hollow trees, crevices under rocks or old burrows, where they are protected from the cold winter weather.

143

Scaly skin

▲ Some snakes have 'keeled' scales, with a raised ridge along the middle of each scale.

322 A snake's skin is protected by a sheet of dry, horny scales that cover its body like a suit of armour. They are made from thick pieces of keratin – the substance that hair, feathers, nails and claws are made from. Snake scales are linked by hinges of thin keratin and usually fold back, overlapping each other.

Head scales

Ventral scales on the underside of the snake's body

Scutes

Dorsal scales on the sides and back

▶ The number, shape, colour and arrangment of a snake's scales helps with identification.

Subcaudal scales under the tail

Scale

Outer layer (epidermis)

Lower layer (dermis)

▲ The areas of skin between a snake's scales allow the body to stretch, making it very flexible.

323 Most snakes have a row of broad scales called scutes underneath their bodies. These scutes go across the snake's belly from one side to the other and end where the tail starts. They help the snake to grip the ground as it moves. Legless lizards don't have scutes, so this is one of the ways to tell them apart from snakes.

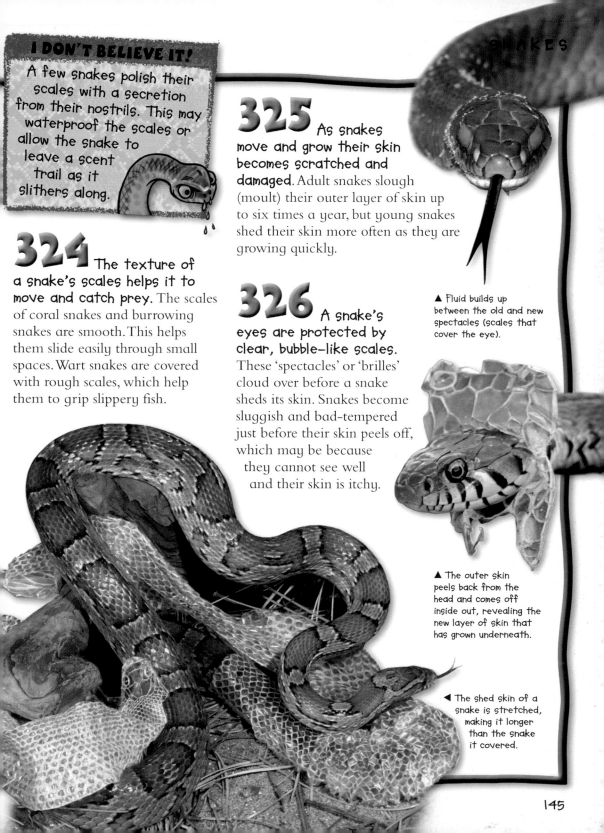

325 As snakes move and grow their skin becomes scratched and damaged. Adult snakes slough (moult) their outer layer of skin up to six times a year, but young snakes shed their skin more often as they are growing quickly.

324 The texture of a snake's scales helps it to move and catch prey. The scales of coral snakes and burrowing snakes are smooth. This helps them slide easily through small spaces. Wart snakes are covered with rough scales, which help them to grip slippery fish.

326 A snake's eyes are protected by clear, bubble-like scales. These 'spectacles' or 'brilles' cloud over before a snake sheds its skin. Snakes become sluggish and bad-tempered just before their skin peels off, which may be because they cannot see well and their skin is itchy.

▲ Fluid builds up between the old and new spectacles (scales that cover the eye).

▲ The outer skin peels back from the head and comes off inside out, revealing the new layer of skin that has grown underneath.

◄ The shed skin of a snake is stretched, making it longer than the snake it covered.

Colours and patterns

327 **Some snakes are brightly coloured to warn predators that they are poisonous.** There are more than 90 species of coral snake, each with a different pattern of red, black and yellow or white bands. Birds have learnt to avoid snakes with these warning colours.

▼ The bright tail of the ring-necked snake distracts predators away from its fragile head.

328 **Some snakes shimmer with rainbow colours.** Snakes in the sunbeam snake family are named after the way their large, smooth, polished scales create a rainbow effect along their bodies. As they move, light strikes the thin, see-through outer layers of their scales, making their colours appear to change.

◄ The scales of the rainbow boa glimmer with different colours.

SNAKE BRACELET

You will need:
thin card   scissors
colouring pencils   hole punch
wool   beads

Cut a strip of card 20 centimetres long and 3 centimetres wide. Use colouring pencils to draw a snake pattern on it. Punch a hole in each end of the card then tie together with strips of wool. Once you have threaded beads onto the wool and tied a knot in each end it is ready to wear.

329 Some snakes use bright colours to startle or threaten predators. Ring-necked snakes are dull colours on top but have brightly coloured bellies. If threatened, this snake will curl its tail into a corkscrew, creating a sudden flash of colour and drawing attention away from its vulnerable head.

◄ The extraordinary nose shield of the leaf-nosed snake may help to camouflage it while it hunts.

330 Many snakes have colours and patterns that make them blend into their surroundings. Their camouflage helps them avoid predators and catch their prey. Patterns on their scales help to break up the outline of their bodies. The patterns on a gaboon viper make it look just like the dead leaves on the floor of an African rainforest.

▼ The gaboon viper is well camouflaged among the leaves as it lies in wait for its prey.

On the move

331 The way a snake moves depends on what species it is, its speed and the surface it is moving over. A snake may wriggle along in an S-shape (serpentine movement), pull half of its body along at a time (concertina movement) or pull its body forwards in a straight line (caterpillar movement).

◀ Tree snakes use an adapted form of concertina movement to move from branch to branch.

332 On smooth or sandy surfaces, snakes move by sidewinding. By anchoring its head and tail firmly on a surface, it can fling the middle part of its body sideways. A sidewinding snake moves diagonally, with only a small part of its body touching the ground at any time.

▼ Sidewinding snakes, such as this viper, leave tracks at a 45° angle to the direction of travel.

333 Tree snakes have strong, prehensile (gripping) tails, which coil around branches. Holding on tightly with its tail, a tree snake stretches forwards to the next branch, and then pulls up its tail. This is a sort of concertina movement.

▲ Large, heavy snakes use their belly scutes to grip the ground and pull themselves forwards.

▲ Most snakes move in an S-shaped path, pushing forwards where their curves touch the ground.

▶ When using concertina movement, a snake bunches up its body (1) then stretches the front half forwards (2), and lastly, pulls up the back half of its body (3).

① ② ③

334 Sea snakes swim using S-shaped wriggles, rather like the serpentine movement used by many land snakes. To give them extra swimming power, sea snakes have broad, flat tails, which push against the water and propel them along.

▼ This high speed photo shows how a paradise tree snake flings its body into the air from a branch to glide for distances of up to 100 metres.

335 A few Asian tree snakes glide through the trees by spreading out their long ribs to create a sort of parachute. This slows down the snakes' fall, so that they float from tree to tree instead of plummeting straight down to the ground.

Super senses

336 Snakes rely on their senses of smell, taste and touch much more than sight or hearing. A snake's tongue is used to collect particles from the air and to touch and feel its surroundings. A snake has a special nerve pit called the Jacobson's organ in the roof of its mouth, which analyses tastes and smells collected by its tongue.

▲ A snake can flick its tongue in and out through a tiny opening even when its mouth is closed. An active snake will do this every few seconds, especially when it is hunting or feels threatened.

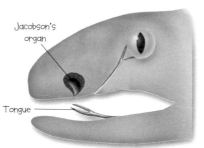

Jacobson's organ

Tongue

◄ A snake's tongue collects scent particles and chemicals from the air and places them in the two openings of the Jacobson's organ in the roof of its mouth.

QUIZ

1. What is the name of the sense organ in the roof of a snake's mouth?
2. What shape are the pupils of snakes that hunt at night?
3. Why do boas and pythons need to sense heat?

Answers:
1. Jacobson's organ 2. Vertical slits 3. They need to detect the warm bodies of their prey

337 Most snakes have well-developed eyes and some have good eyesight. Some tree snakes have a groove along the snout in front of each of their eyes, so they can see forwards to judge depth and distance. Coachwhip snakes are one of the few snakes to hunt mainly by sight, raising the front end parts of their bodies off the ground.

338 Day-hunting snakes usually have round pupils, whereas night-hunting snakes have vertical, slit-shaped pupils. Vertical pupils can be closed more tightly than round ones, helping protect the snake's eyes from bright light when it comes out to bask in the Sun during the day.

▶ The day-hunting oriental whip snake has a distinctive keyhole-shaped pupil.

▶ The round pupil of a Natal green snake is surrounded by a beautiful golden iris.

▶ The eyelash viper has the typical slit-shaped pupil of a night-hunting snake.

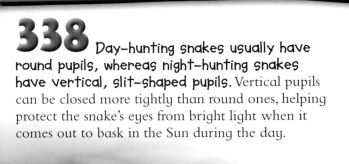

▼ By looking along grooves in its narrow, pointed snout, a vine snake can focus both eyes at once, giving it 3D vision.

339 Snakes have no outer ears or eardrums so they cannot hear sounds in the same way we do. They have an inner ear bone connected to the jaw, which helps them to sense ground vibrations. A snake can also pick up vibrations from the air through its skin.

Heat pits

340 Some snakes, such as pit vipers, boas and pythons, are able to sense the heat given off by their prey. They are the only animals that can do this and their unique sense allows them to track warm-blooded prey, such as rats, in the dark.

◀ Vipers have holes behind their nostrils that are lined with heat-sensitive cells. Boas and pythons have similar heat holes along their lips.

Hunting and eating

341 Most snakes eat a wide variety of prey depending on their size, the season and what is available. But a few snakes have very specific diets. Thirst snakes feed only on slugs and snails, queen snakes eat crayfish and children's pythons can move fast enough to catch bats.

▶ The common kingsnake can eat poisonous snakes. It can digest the venom so it is not harmed.

◀ The jaws of an egg-eating snake stretch to swallow an egg three times the diameter of its head.

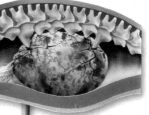

◀ Once the egg has been swallowed, the snake arches its neck, forcing pointed bones in its throat to break through the shell.

◀ The snake then swallows the egg's nutritious contents, and regurgitates (coughs up) the crushed eggshell.

342 An egg-eating snake swallows eggs whole and uses the pointed ends of bones that jut into its throat to crack open the shell. Eggs are a useful source of food because they are rich in body-building protein as well as being easy to find.

I DON'T BELIEVE IT!

Large snakes can swallow prey up to a quarter of their own length. They have been known to eat leopards, gazelles and even small crocodiles!

344 Many snakes lie in wait to ambush their prey because they cannot move fast enough to chase after it. Snakes such as vipers, boas and pythons have wide bodies so they can eat big meals. They do not have breastbones, so they can move their ribs apart at the front to make their bodies even wider.

345 Some snakes, such as the king cobra, even eat other snakes! A snake's body is easier to swallow than other prey, such as mammals or birds, because it is a thin, smooth shape. Most snakes that eat poisonous snakes are immune to their poisons.

▼ Young Mexican cantils have a bright green or yellow tip to their tail. They use this to lure prey, such as frogs, lizards or rodents.

343 Some snakes set traps for their prey. The death adder has a brightly coloured tip to its tail, which looks similar to a worm. The adder wriggles this 'worm' to lure lizards, birds and worms within reach of its poisonous jaws.

155

Teeth and jaws

346 **Most snakes have short, sharp, curved teeth to grip and hold their prey.** The teeth are no good for chewing or tearing up food, which is why snakes swallow their prey whole. A snake's teeth often break as it feeds, but new teeth grow to replace broken ones.

347 **Many smaller snakes swallow prey alive, but larger snakes kill their food before they eat it.** Around 700 species of snakes use poison, called venom, to immobilize or kill their prey. The venom is injected into the prey through large, pointed teeth, called fangs, which are connected to glands (bags) of venom in the snake's head.

▶ Rear-fanged snakes need to chew their venom into their prey for 15 minutes or more before the poison takes effect.

Fangs are towards the rear of the mouth, below the eye

348 **Snakes can have fangs at the front or back of their mouths.** Some fanged snakes, such as vipers and cobras, have fangs at the front, while a few snakes, such as the African boomslang, have fangs at the back. Back fangs may either just be large back teeth, or they may have grooves for venom.

▼ Fangs at the back of a snake's mouth help to kill prey as it is being swallowed.

◄ The large fangs of an eyelash viper swing forward to inject venom into its prey.

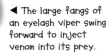

TRUE OR FALSE?

1. A snake can grow new teeth to replace broken ones.
2. Snake poison is called mevon.
3. Vipers have fangs that can be folded back when they are not being used.

Answers:
1. True 2. False – it is called venom 3. True

349 Snakes in the viper family, such as rattlesnakes and eyelash vipers, have moveable fangs. These can be folded back against the roof of the mouth when they are not in use. When the snake strikes, the fangs swing forwards and bite into the prey, injecting venom deep inside the victim's body.

◄ Most poisonous snakes have hollow fangs at the front of their mouth.

► The puff adder has long, folding fangs and strong venom. It is Africa's most dangerous snake.

350 Snakes can open their mouths wider than any other animal, thanks to hinged bones and a stretchy ligament joining the top and bottom jaws. The two sides of a snake's jaw can also move independently of each other, allowing the snake to 'walk' its jaws from side to side as it forces food down its throat, with first one side pulling and then the other.

► The red arrow shows how the lower jaw is attached to the skull like a hinge, allowing the jaw to open widely. The blue arrows show how the two sides of the jaw can move backwards and forwards separately.

The lower jaw can stretch wide apart because it is in two halves, joined at the front by a stretchy ligament

Poisonous snakes

351 **Venom is a highly modified form of saliva (spit).** Saliva is a type of digestive juice, so venom contains enzymes (particles that break down food). These start to digest and soften the meal even before the snake has swallowed it. Snakes don't run out of venom, because their glands make more poison as they use it up.

▶ Eyelash vipers catch prey while hanging from tree branches. Small animals are overcome by venom in minutes.

VENOM KEY

① Venom gland sits in the side of the snake's head

② A tube leads from the gland down to the fangs

③ Fangs are hollow with a venom canal down the middle

④ Venom is injected deep into the prey's muscle tissue

352 **Snake venom is a complicated substance that works in two main ways.** Snakes such as cobras, coral snakes and sea snakes have venom that attacks the victim's nervous system, causing paralysis (stopping all movement) and preventing breathing. Snakes such as vipers have venom that destroys body tissues, attacking the circulatory system (blood vessels) and muscles.

353 Venom is useful because it allows snakes to overcome their prey quickly without being injured. Snakes with powerful venom, such as vipers, tend to bite their prey quickly and then retreat to a place of safety while their poison takes effect. If the victim crawls away to die, the snake follows its scent trail to keep track of its meal.

▲ The venom of the common krait is very powerful — these snakes are even more poisonous than common cobras.

▼ As the snake bites down, venom flows down its fangs and can be collected in the bottom of a jar.

354 If a person is biten by a venomous snake the deadliness of the bite varies. The size and health of the victim, the size of the snake, the number of bites, the amount of venom injected and the speed and quality of medical treatment are important. Some of the most dangerous snakes in the world are the black mamba, Russell's viper and the beaked sea snake.

▶ The black mamba is the longest venomous snake in Africa and is named after the black colour inside its mouth, which it displays if threatened.

355 Venom is collected from poisonous snakes by making them bite down on the top of a jar. The venom is used to make a medicine called antivenin, which helps people recover from snake bites. Snake venom can also be used to make other medicines that treat high blood pressure, heart failure and kidney disease.

I DON'T BELIEVE IT!
The king cobra is the world's longest venomous snake, growing to lengths of over 5.4 metres. Its venom is powerful enough to kill an elephant!

Cobras and vipers

356 **The two main groups of poisonous snakes are vipers and elapids.** The cobras of Africa and Asia belong to the elapid family, as do the colourful coral snakes of the Americas and the mambas of Africa. Elapids have short, fixed fangs at the front of their mouths, as do their relatives, the sea snakes.

357 **Cobras can spread out the skin around their neck into a wide 'hood' that makes them look larger and frightening to their attackers.** The hood is supported by , movable ribs in the cobra's neck. Some cobras have huge eye-spots on the back of the hood, which probably startle predators.

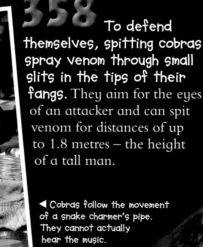

358 **To defend themselves, spitting cobras spray venom through small slits in the tips of their fangs.** They aim for the eyes of an attacker and can spit venom for distances of up to 1.8 metres – the height of a tall man.

◄ Cobras follow the movement of a snake charmer's pipe. They cannot actually hear the music.

▼ Spitting cobras spray their venom by pushing air out of their lungs while forcing the venom through holes in the front of their fangs.

359 The viper family of venomous snakes includes the adders, night adders, vipers, bush vipers, rattlesnakes, copperheads, asps and pit vipers. All vipers have long, hollow fangs that can be folded back inside their mouths. The largest viper is the bushmaster, which lives in the forests of Central and South America and grows up to 3.6 metres in length.

▼ The palm viper lives in trees and shrubs, often at the base of palm fronds. Its prehensile tail acts as an anchor.

360 The puff adder inflates its lungs when threatened, which makes its body puff up like a balloon, making it look bigger than it really is. The saw-scaled viper is also named after its threat display because it makes a rasping sound with its jagged-edged scales.

Crushing coils

361 Snakes that squeeze their prey to death by wrapping it tightly in their strong coils are called constrictors. All boas and pythons are constrictors, as are the sunbeam snakes and some of the snakes in the colubrid family, such as rat snakes and kingsnakes.

▼ 1. The snake holds its prey in its teeth and squeezes it to death in its strong coils.

▲ 2. When the animal is dead, the snake opens its mouth very wide and starts to swallow its meal.

362 Constricting snakes usually hold the head end of their prey with their sharp teeth. They then throw their coils around the animal's body and squeeze hard to stop it from breathing. Each time the victim breathes out, the snake squeezes a little harder, until it dies from suffocation or shock.

363 The time it takes for the snake's prey to die depends on the size of the prey and how strong it is. When the prey stops struggling, the snake relaxes its grip, unhinges its jaws and starts to force its meal down its throat.

364 Prey is usually swallowed head–first. The legs or wings of the animal fold back against the sides of the body and the fur or feathers lie flat – making it easier for the snake to swallow. Slimy saliva in the snake's mouth helps the prey to slide down its throat and into its stomach.

365 When it is swallowing a large meal, a snake finds it difficult to breathe. It may take a long time to swallow a big animal. The snake moves the opening of its windpipe to the front of its mouth so that it can keep breathing while it swallows.

▼ 3. A snake's meal forms a bulge in the middle of its body while it is being digested. It may take days, or even weeks, to be absorbed completely.

Boas and pythons

366 Two powerful types of constricting snakes are boas and pythons. Unlike many other types of snake, most of them have a working left lung, hip bones and the remains of back leg bones. Many boas and pythons have heat-sensitive jaw pits to detect their prey.

367 Many boas and pythons have markings that give them excellent camouflage. The patterns help them to lie in wait for their prey without being seen. The sand boa perfectly matches the rocks and sand of its desert habitat.

▲ The shape of the Kenyan sand boa's mouth and jaws helps it to dig through soft sand.

368 The ball python, or royal python, from West Africa, coils into a tight ball when it is threatened. Its head is well protected in the middle of its coils and it can even be rolled along the ground in this position.

▶ A ball python in a defensive ball shows off its camouflage colours. These snakes can live for up to 50 years.

369

The emerald tree boa and the green tree python look alike. These two snakes live in different parts of the world and are not closely related, but they look and behave in a similar way because they both live in rainforest environments.

Emerald tree boa

▲▼ Emerald tree boas and green tree pythons rest in the same way, coiled around branches. They grip tightly with their prehensile tails.

370

Boas and pythons live in different places around the world. Most boas live in Central and South America, while pythons live in Africa, southeast Asia and Australia. Another difference between the two snake groups is that all boas (except for one species) give birth to live young, while all pythons lay eggs.

I DON'T BELIEVE IT!
The smallest type of python in the world is the anthill python, which grows to a maximum length of 30 centimetres.

Green tree python

Survival skills

371 Snakes have delicate bodies and are vulnerable to attack from a variety of predators. Animals such as foxes, racoons, crocodiles, baboons and even other snakes will attack them. Predators that specialize in snakes include the secretary bird of the African grasslands, which stamps on snakes to kill them.

372 Rattlesnakes warn predators to keep away by shaking the hollow scales on their tails, making a buzzing sound. Each time a rattlesnake sheds its skin, an extra section of the tail remains, making its rattle one section longer.

◀ A rattlesnake's 'rattle' is a chain of hollow tail tips, which make a warning sound when shaken.

373 Most predators prefer to eat live prey, so the hognose snake and the grass snake pretend to be dead if they are attacked. They roll onto their backs, open their mouths and keep very still until the predator goes away.

▲ Some snakes 'play dead' to trick a predator into leaving them alone.

374

The harmless milk snake copies the colour pattern of the venomous coral snake. The two snakes look so similar that predators can't tell the difference between them, and leave the milk snake alone.

Coral snake

Milk snake

◀ A mongoose is agile enough to kill snakes such as cobras. It is partly immune to the venom and is protected by its thick fur coat.

375

Spraying smelly liquid at a predator, or smearing itself with an unpleasant scent, is a good way for a snake to escape attack. Many snakes, such as the cottonmouth, the hognose snake and the Chinese stink snake, give off a nasty-smelling yellow or green fluid when they are picked up or attacked.

QUIZ

1. What is the 'rattle' on a rattlesnake's tail made of?
2. Which African bird kills snakes by stamping on them?
3. Which of these two snakes is venomous – the milk snake or the coral snake?

Answers:
1. The rattle is made of hollow scales 2. The secretary bird 3. The coral snake is venomous

Courtship

376 At certain times of year, usually in the spring or the rainy season, mature male and female snakes search for a mate. They are ready to mate when they are between two and five years old. Male snakes find females by following their scent trails, which signal that they are ready to mate.

▶ Blue-banded sea snakes stay close to each other during courtship and females give birth to between three and five young in the water. The young can swim and feed as soon as they are born.

377 Male boas and pythons have small spurs on the ends of their tiny back leg bones. They use these spurs to tickle the females during courtship, and also to fight with other males. Females may also have spurs, but these are usually smaller than the spurs of the males.

378
Many snakes mate when they emerge from hibernation in spring. Male garter snakes emerge from hibernation first so they can warm up in the Sun and be ready to compete for the females when they emerge.

▲ During courtship, a male red-sided garter snake lies with its body pressed closely against the female and presses its chin against her head.

379
Rival male snakes of some species, such as adders, mambas, vipers and some rattlesnakes, compete for females in a test of strength that is rather like a wrestling match. They coil around each other, sometimes rearing up into the air, and try to push each other down to the ground. These tests of strength can last for hours.

▶ A fighting male rattlesnake sways to and fro, looking for a chance to coil his body around the rival and pin him to the ground.

380
Female flowerpot snakes are believed to be able to produce baby snakes without mating with males, using a form of reproduction known as 'parthenogenesis'. All the young produced in this way are females, but they can reproduce clones of themselves when the conditions are ideal, without having to wait for a male.

167

Laying eggs

381
About 80 percent of snakes reproduce by laying eggs. A snake's eggshell is tough, leathery, flexible and almost water-tight, protecting the developing baby inside from drying out. Female snakes usually lay about five to 20 eggs at a time.

382
Most female snakes don't look after their eggs once they have been laid. Only a few, such as the bushmaster snake, some cobras and most pythons, stay with their eggs to protect them from predators and bad weather.

▼ This cutaway artwork shows a female Burmese python laying eggs. She may lay up to 100 eggs in a single clutch (batch).

383
The female king cobra is the only snake known to make a nest for her eggs. She builds a mound of rotten leaves, twigs and plant material, lays her eggs in the middle and then perches on top to prevent predators, such as wild boars, from eating them.

384 Female grass snakes and rat snakes lay their eggs in compost heaps or manure heaps. The warmth given off by the rotting plants helps to speed up the development of their eggs.

▲ The grass snake is the only snake in Britain that lays eggs. Females lay 10–40 eggs at a time.

① When fully developed, a baby snake uses the egg tooth on the tip of its snout to tear a hole in the egg.

② The snake tastes the air with its forked tongue. It may stay in the shell for a few days.

③ Eventually, the snake decides to uncoil its slim body and begins to wriggle free of the egg.

385 Baby snakes develop inside eggs for six to 12 weeks, feeding on the yolk stored inside. When it is ready to hatch, a baby snake makes a slit in the eggshell with a sharp egg tooth on its snout. A few hours after hatching, the egg tooth drops off.

④ The baby snake slides along in S-shaped curves to begin its life in the wild.

Giving birth

386
About 20 percent of all snakes give birth to live babies. Boas, rattlesnakes, garter snakes and adders don't lay eggs. Instead, the babies develop inside the mother, and are contained inside clear, tough sacs called membranes instead of shells.

▶ Baby eyelash vipers are about 15–18 centimetres long when they are born. They stay with their mother for about two weeks until they moult their skin for the first time.

The babies have white tips to their tails to lure prey close enough for them to capture

387
Snakes that give birth to live young often live in cold climates. The warmth inside the mother's body helps the baby snakes to develop. The mother can also look for warm places to soak up the Sun's heat, which speeds up the development of her young.

388 Baby snakes that develop inside their mother are better protected than eggs that are laid on the ground. A pregnant snake is heavy, so she often hides away to avoid predators. The extra weight of her developing babies also makes it harder for her to chase prey.

389 Most sea snakes usually give birth to live young, which means they do not have to come onto land to lay eggs. The baby sea snakes are born underwater and have to swim up to the surface to take their first breath. Yellow-bellied sea snakes breed in warm oceans and females give birth to between one and 10 young after five to six months.

390 Most snakes that give birth to live young do not look after their babies when they are born. Venomous snakes are born with their venom glands full of poison, so they can give a dangerous bite to predators soon after birth.

Myths and legends

391 **In ancient Greek mythology the hair of the monster Medusa was made of snakes.** Anyone who looked at her was instantly turned to stone. The hero Perseus was able to cut off Medusa's head by looking at her reflection in his shield. The drops of blood that fell from the head turned into vipers!

◀ Gilgamesh was probably the ruler of the city of Uruk, from which modern-day Iraq gets its name.

392 **In a poem from the Middle East about the hero Gilgamesh, a snake ate a magic plant that could make a person young again.** Ever since, so the story goes, snakes have shed their skin and become young again.

▲ Medusa's hair was said to have been turned to snakes as a punishment by the Greek goddess Athena.

393 **In the Bible, a serpent in the Garden of Eden persuaded Eve, the first woman, to eat forbidden fruit.** Eve gave some of the fruit from the Tree of the Knowledge of Good and Evil to Adam, the first man. God made them leave the Garden of Eden as a punishment.

▲ The serpent told Eve that eating the apple would make her as wise and powerful as God.

QUIZ

1. Medusa's hair is made of ropes.
2. Heracles was very good at killing snakes.
3. The story of the rainbow serpent comes from Africa.

Answers:
1. False, Medusa's hair is made of snakes. 2. True 3. False, the story of the rainbow serpent comes from Australia

394 Heracles
was the son of Zeus, king of
the ancient Greek gods.
Legend says he strangled two
snakes with his bare hands
when he was just a baby. The
two snakes were sent to kill him
by Zeus' jealous wife, Hera, who
was not his mother.

395 Traditional beliefs
in Australia, India, North
America and Africa have linked
snakes with rainbows. Rainbows
are often associated with rain and
new life in different cultures. The Hopi
Indians of North America used living snakes
in their rain dances and the ancient Chinese
also connected snakes with life-giving rain.

▲ The legendary hero Heracles
killed a monster called the Hydra.
This snake-like creature had nine
heads, one of which was immortal.

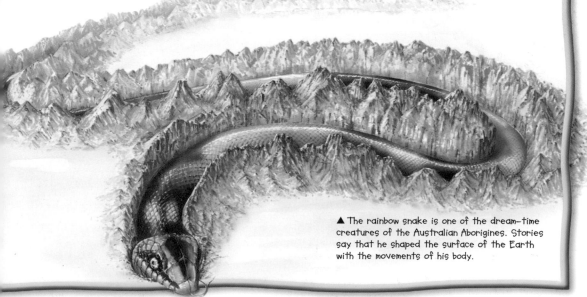

▲ The rainbow snake is one of the dream-time
creatures of the Australian Aborigines. Stories
say that he shaped the surface of the Earth
with the movements of his body.

Save our snakes!

396 The biggest threat to snakes comes from humans who are destroying their natural habitats. Many snakes are killed by cars and trucks on the road. They are also killed to make tourist souvenirs or for use in traditional medicines.

▲ Some snakes are used to make traditional medicines by soaking them in rice wine, or another type of alcohol.

397 One reason snakes are important is because they control insect and rat populations. To find out the best ways of protecting and conserving snakes, scientists fit them with radio transmitters or tags to mark individuals and collect data about their secretive lives.

▼ Radio-tracking snakes helps conservationists work out why a species is becoming rare and to plan the management of wildlife parks.

398 During the Hindu festival of Nagpanchami, thousands of snakes have traditionally been trapped and killed. Volunteers now rescue the snakes, which are protected by Indian law, and return them to the wild if possible.

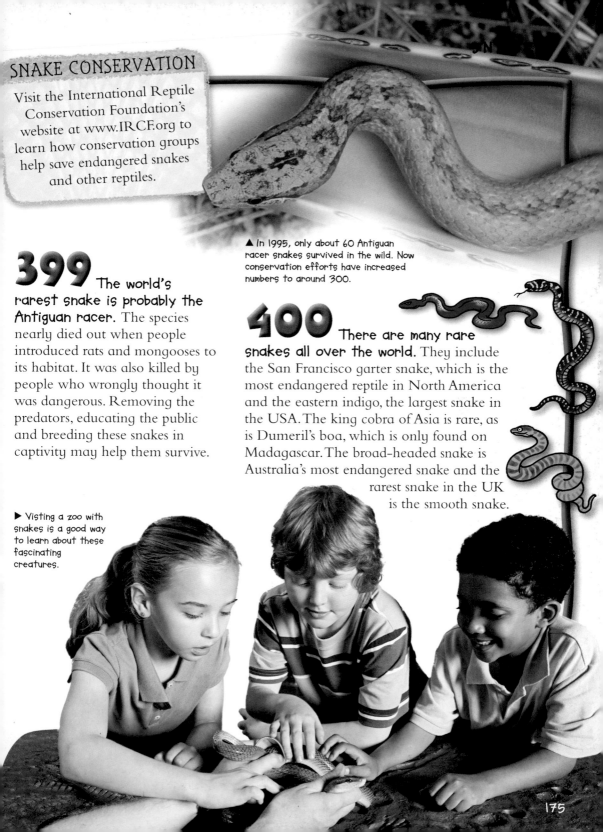

SNAKE CONSERVATION

Visit the International Reptile Conservation Foundation's website at www.IRCF.org to learn how conservation groups help save endangered snakes and other reptiles.

▲ In 1995, only about 60 Antiguan racer snakes survived in the wild. Now conservation efforts have increased numbers to around 300.

399 The world's rarest snake is probably the Antiguan racer. The species nearly died out when people introduced rats and mongooses to its habitat. It was also killed by people who wrongly thought it was dangerous. Removing the predators, educating the public and breeding these snakes in captivity may help them survive.

400 There are many rare snakes all over the world. They include the San Francisco garter snake, which is the most endangered reptile in North America and the eastern indigo, the largest snake in the USA. The king cobra of Asia is rare, as is Dumeril's boa, which is only found on Madagascar. The broad-headed snake is Australia's most endangered snake and the rarest snake in the UK is the smooth snake.

▶ Visting a zoo with snakes is a good way to learn about these fascinating creatures.

A fight to survive

401 **The world is full of animals that are fighting to survive.** There are many reasons why animals may attack one another. Some are called predators and they kill for food. Others only kill to defend themselves, their young or their homes. Whatever the reason for using their claws, jaws, poisons or stings, these creatures are fascinating, but deadly.

▼ To catch its prey, the Nile crocodile lies very still in the water until the gazelle comes close. Then it shoots out of its hiding place, trying to catch the gazelle in its powerful jaws.

Killer carnivores

◀ False vampire bats have very sharp teeth, like the vampire bat. They catch and feed on frogs, mice, birds and other bats.

402 **Animals that eat meat are called carnivores.** Scavengers are carnivores that steal meat from others, or find dead animals to eat. Most carnivores, however, have to hunt and kill. These animals are called predators.

403 **Killer whales are some of the largest predators in the world.** Despite their size, these mighty beasts often hunt in groups called pods. By working together, killer whales can kill large animals, including other whales. However, they usually hunt smaller creatures, such as sea lions and dolphins.

▼ Anacondas are types of boa, and are the heaviest snakes in the world. As they don't have chewing teeth, snakes swallow their prey whole. Anacondas feed on large rodents called capybara, deer, fish and birds.

404 **Vampire bats do not eat meat, but they do feed on other animals.** With their razor-sharp teeth, vampire bats pierce the skin of a sleeping animal, such as a horse or pig, and drink their blood. False vampire bats are bigger, and they eat the flesh of other animals.

405 With their cold eyes and gaping mouths, piranhas are fierce-looking predators. When a shoal, or group, of piranhas attack, they work together like an enormous slicing machine. Within minutes, they can strip a horse to its skeleton using their tiny triangular teeth.

▲ Red piranhas are aggressive, speedy predators. They work together in a group to attack their prey, such as birds.

406 Some snakes rely on venom, or poison, to kill their prey, but constrictors squeeze their victims to death. Pythons and boas wrap their enormous bodies around the victim. Every time the captured animal breathes out, the snake squeezes a little tighter, until its prey can no longer breathe.

Lethal weapons

407 Many animals have deadly weapons, including teeth, claws, horns and stings. They are perfect for killing prey, or fighting enemies.

408 Inside the mouth of a meat-eating predator is an impressive collection of deadly daggers — teeth. Different teeth do different jobs. Canines, or fangs, are long and knife-like, and are used to grab prey or pierce skin. Teeth at the front of the mouth are very sharp, and are ideal for cutting and slicing flesh.

◀ Mandrills are part of the same family as monkeys, called primates. Males bare their enormous fangs when they are anxious, or want to scare other males. The fangs may reach up to 7 centimetres in length.

409 Stings are common weapons in the animal world and they are used by creatures such as jellyfish and scorpions. Stings usually contain poison, or venom. The stingray, for example, is a fish with a long saw-shaped spine on its tail, which is coated in poison.

410

Elephant and walrus tusks are overgrown teeth that make fearsome weapons when used to stab and lunge at attackers. Males use their tusks to fight one another at mating time, or to scare away predators. An elephant can kill a person with a single thrust from its mighty tusks.

FIND YOUR FANGS

You have cutting and chewing teeth, too. Use a mirror to find them.

Incisors are the sharp, flat teeth at the front of your mouth. They are used for cutting and tearing food.

Canines are the pointy teeth next to the incisors, used for piercing food.

Molars are at the back of your mouth. They are used for grinding food.

▼ Birds of prey grab hold of their victim with powerful talons, which pierce the flesh with ease.

▼ Cats have sharp claws that can be pulled back into the paws when they are not being used.

412

Some animals fight for mates, or territory (the area they live in). Horned animals, such as deer, are not predators, but they may fight and attack other animals. These animals have been known to harm humans when they are scared.

411

Eagles have huge claws called talons. The bird grasps prey in its feet, killing it by piercing and squeezing with its talons. Eagles and other carnivorous (meat-eating) birds are called birds of prey.

▲ Ibex are wild goats. They use their thick, curved horns to fight for mates or territory. Horns can be used to stab, wound and even kill.

Silent hunters

413 Agile and fast, with sharp teeth and claws, cats are some of the deadliest predators in the world. Most cats hunt alone, but lions works as a team to catch their prey.

414 A group of lions is called a pride, and the females are the hunters. Cubs spend hours play-fighting. This helps them to practise the skills they will need to catch and kill prey when they are older.

415 In Asia, many people are fearful of living near tigers. However, tigers hunt small creatures, such as birds, monkeys and reptiles. They have been known to attack bigger animals, such as rhinos and elephants, but it is rare for them to kill humans.

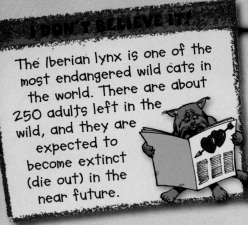

The Iberian lynx is one of the most endangered wild cats in the world. There are about 250 adults left in the wild, and they are expected to become extinct (die out) in the near future.

▼ Lionesses hunt in a group, which means they can attack big, aggressive animals, such as buffaloes.

416 Cheetahs are the fastest hunters on land, and can reach speeds of more than 100 kilometres an hour. Despite their great speed, cheetahs often fail to catch the animal they are chasing. Although these cats have great spurts of energy, they tire very quickly. If cheetahs have not caught their prey in about 30 seconds, it may escape – this time.

417 Leopards are secretive killers. They live throughout Africa and Asia, but are rarely seen. They are agile climbers and spend much of their time in trees, waiting for unsuspecting animals to wander by. Like most cats, leopards kill prey by sinking their huge teeth into the victim's neck.

Big, bold, and beastly

▶ Polar bears are meat eaters. They wait by a seal's breathing hole for the seal to appear above the water. With one swift bite, the bear kills its prey, drags it out of the water and begins to feast.

418 Big, white and fluffy, polar bears look cuddly, but they are deadly predators. Occasionally, polar bears travel from the icy Arctic to small towns in search of food. At these times, they are hungry and dangerous, and may attack.

▼ A polar bear's paw is as big as a dinner plate, and is equipped with five big claws, one on each toe.

419 Polar bears use their huge paws to swim with ease underwater. They can hold their breath for several minutes, waiting until the time is right to swim up and grab their prey. On land, these ferocious bears hunt by creeping up on their prey, then pouncing, leaving the victim with no escape.

421 Grizzlies are brown bears of North America. They often come into contact with humans when searching for food and raiding rubbish bins, and are considered to be extremely dangerous. Grizzlies often live in woods and forests. They mainly feed on berries, fruit, bulbs and roots, but also fish for salmon in fast-flowing rivers.

▲ Kodiak bears live in Alaska where they eat fish, grass, plants and berries. They only bare their teeth and roar to defend themselves against predators.

422 Black bears in Asia rarely attack humans, but when they do, the attack is often fatal. Asian black bears are herbivores. This means that they eat plants rather than meat. If they are scared, these shy animals may attack to kill.

420 Brown bears are one of the largest meat eaters in the world, and can stand more than 3 metres tall. They are powerful animals, with long front claws and strong jaws.

▶ Brown bears catch salmon as they leap out of the water. A snap of the jaws is enough to grab the wriggling fish.

Skills to kill

423 Monkeys and apes belong to the same group of animals as humans, called primates. These intelligent creatures have great skills of communication and teamwork. Although monkeys, gorillas and chimps appear to be playful, they can be dangerous.

424 It was once believed that chimps only ate plants and insects. However, it has been discovered that groups of chimps ambush and attack colobus monkeys. Each chimp takes its own role in the hunting team. During the chase, the chimps communicate with each other by screeching and hooting.

425 Chimps also kill each other. Groups of male chimps patrol the forest, looking for males from another area. If they find one, the group may gang up on the stranger and kill him.

▶ Chimps use their great intelligence to organize hunts. Some of them scream, hoot and chase the colobus monkey. Other chimps in the group hide, ready to attack.

426 Baboons live in family groups and eat a wide range of foods, from seeds to antelopes. Young males eventually leave their family, and fight with other males to join a new group and find mates.

427 A mighty gorilla may seem fierce, but it is actually one of the most gentle primates. Large adult males, called silverbacks, only charge to protect their families by scaring other animals, or humans, away. Gorillas can inflict terrible bite wounds with their fearsome fangs.

I DON'T BELIEVE IT!

Chimps are skilled at making and using tools. It is easy for them to hold sticks and rocks in their hands. They use sticks to break open insects' nests and they use rocks to smash nuts.

Canine killers

428 Wolves, coyotes and African hunting dogs belong to the dog family. Most live and hunt in groups, or packs. By working together, a pack can attack and kill large prey, such as deer and bison.

◀ When a wolf feels threatened, the fur on its back, called its hackles, stands on end. This makes it look bigger and fiercer.

429 Wolves have excellent senses of sight, hearing and smell to help them to find their prey. These strong, agile creatures have been known to travel a distance of 100 kilometres in just one night in search of food.

430 Coyotes are wild dogs that live in North America. They normally hunt in pairs or on their own, although they may join together as a group to chase large prey, such as deer.

431
Like wild cats, coyotes hunt by keeping still and watching an animal nearby. They wait for the right moment, then creep towards their prey and pounce, landing on top of the startled victim. Coyotes are swift runners and often chase jackrabbits across rocks and up hills.

BE A WOLF!

1. One person is Mr Wolf and stands with their back to the other players.
2. The players stand 10 paces away and shout, "What's the time, Mr Wolf?".
3. If Mr Wolf shouts, "It's 10 o'clock", the players take 10 steps towards Mr Wolf.
4. Watch out because when Mr Wolf shouts "Dinnertime", he chases the other players and whoever he catches is out of the game!

▼ When African hunting dogs pursue their prey, such as the wildebeest, the chase may go on for several kilometres, but the dogs rarely give up. They wait until their prey tires, then leap in for the kill.

432
African wild dogs are deadly pack hunters. They work as a team to chase and torment their prey. The whole pack shares the meal, tearing at the meat with their sharp teeth.

Ambush and attack

433 Lurking beneath the surface of the water, a deadly hunter waits, ready to pounce. Lying absolutely still, only its eyes and nostrils are visible. With one swift movement, the victim is dragged underwater. This killer is the crocodile, a relative of the dinosaurs.

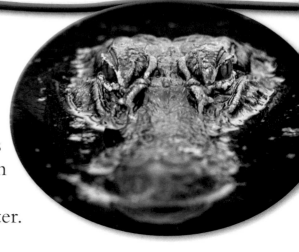

▲ Crocodiles and alligators are well-suited to their aquatic lifestyle. They spend much of their day in water, keeping cool and hidden from view.

Only teeth in the upper jaw are visible

Alligator

▲▼ When a crocodile's mouth is closed, some of the teeth on its lower jaw can be seen. Alligators have wide u-shaped jaws, but the jaws of crocodiles are narrow and v-shaped.

Teeth in the lower jaw can be seen

Crocodile

434 When a crocodile has its prey in sight, it moves at lightning speed. The prey has little chance to escape as the crocodile pulls it underwater. Gripping the victim in its mighty jaws, the crocodile twists and turns in a 'deathspin' until its victim has drowned.

435 The largest crocodiles in the world live in estuaries, where rivers meet the oceans. They are called estuarine crocodiles and can reach a staggering 7 metres in length. These giant predators are often known as man-eating crocodiles, although they are most likely to catch turtles, snakes, monkeys, cows and pigs.

436

Alligators are very strong reptiles with wide jaws and thick, scaly skin on their backs. They live in marshes, ponds and rivers, often close to where people live. Like all crocodiles and alligators, the American alligator will catch and eat anything. They have even been known to attack humans.

▼ Crocodiles and alligators have huge jaws, full of teeth. As well as being used for grabbing and holding prey, they use their teeth to slice pieces from the body of the victim.

I DON'T BELIEVE IT!

Crocodiles and alligators store their uneaten food underwater for several weeks. The remains rot, making it easier for the reptiles to swallow. Yum!

Ravenous raptors

437 Eagles, hawks, kites and ospreys are fearsome predators called birds of prey. Equipped with incredible eyesight, powerful legs, and sharp claws and bills, they hunt during the day, soaring high in the sky as they look for food.

438 Birds of prey are also known as raptors, which comes from the Latin word 'rapere', meaning 'to seize'. Once they have captured their prey, such as a mouse, bird or frog, a raptor usually takes it to its nest to start pulling off fur and feathers. Bones are also thrown away, and the ground near a raptor's nest may be strewn with animal remains.

▶ Like most birds of prey, golden eagles have razor–sharp, hooked bills. They use them to tear the body of their prey apart.

▶ Eagle owls are large, powerful birds. They hunt and capture large animals, including other owls and birds of prey.

439 Birds do not have teeth. They have bills, or beaks, instead. Tearing large pieces of meat is a difficult job using just a bill. Birds of prey use their curved claws, called talons, to hold or rip their food apart, or they just swallow it whole.

440 Little more than the flap of a wing can be heard as an owl swoops down to grab an unsuspecting mouse. Owls hunt at night. They can even see small movements on the ground, thanks to their large eyes and sharp eyesight. When they hunt in total darkness, they rely on their excellent sense of hearing to find food.

QUIZ

The names of raptors have been jumbled up. Can you work out what they are?

1. GELEA
2. ITKE
3. CFALNO
4. LOW
5. PRYESO
6. KAWH

Answers:
1. Eagle 2. Kite 3. Falcon 4. Owl 5. Osprey 6. Hawk

441 **Peregrine falcons are the fastest hunters in the world, reaching speeds of up to 230 kilometres an hour as they swoop down to attack other birds.** Peregrines hunt on the wing. This means that they catch their prey while in flight. They chase their prey to tire it out, before lashing out with their sharp talons.

▼ Bald eagles live on a diet of fish, which they swipe out of the water using their talons.

442 **Ospreys dive, feet-first, into the water from a great height in pursuit of their prey.** Fish may be slippery, but ospreys have spiky scales on the underside of the feet so they can grip more easily. Once ospreys have a fish firmly in their grasp, they fly away to find a safe place to eat.

193

Mighty monsters

443 Not all deadly creatures kill for food. Many of them only attack when they are frightened. Some plant-eating animals fight to protect their young, or when they feel scared.

444 Hippos may appear calm when they are wallowing at the edge of a waterhole, but they kill more people in Africa than any other large animal. These huge creatures fiercely protect their own stretch of water, and females are extremely aggressive when they have calves and feel threatened.

445 African buffaloes can be very aggressive towards other animals and humans. If they become scared, they move quickly and attack with their huge horns. Groups of buffaloes surround a calf or ill member of the herd to protect it. They face outwards to prevent predators getting too close.

446 If an elephant starts flapping its ears and trumpeting, it is giving a warning sign to stay away. However, when an elephant folds its ears back, curls its trunk under its mouth and begins to run – then it really means business. Elephants will attack to keep other animals or humans away from the infants in their herd, and males will fight one another for a mate.

447 With huge bodies and massive horns, rhinos look like fearsome predators. They are actually related to horses and eat a diet of leaves, grass and fruit. Rhinos can become aggressive, however, when they are scared. They have poor eyesight, which may be why they can easily feel confused or threatened, and attack without warning.

◄ Male hippos fight one another using their massive teeth as weapons. Severe injuries can occur, leading to the death of at least one of the hippos.

I DON'T BELIEVE IT!

Adult male elephants are called bulls, and they can become killers. A single stab from an elephant's tusk is enough to cause a fatal wound, and one elephant is strong enough to flip a car over onto its side!

Toxic tools

▶ Marine toads are the largest toads in the world. When they are threatened, venom oozes from the glands in the toad's skin. This poison could kill a small animal in minutes.

448 Some animals rely on teeth and claws to kill prey, but others have an even deadlier weapon called venom. Venom is the name given to any poison that is made by an animal's body. There are lots of different types of venom. Some cause only a painful sting, but others can result in death.

▼ The death stalker scorpion is one of the most dangerous scorpions in the world. It lives in North Africa and the Middle East. One sting can cause paralysis (loss of movement) and heart failure in humans.

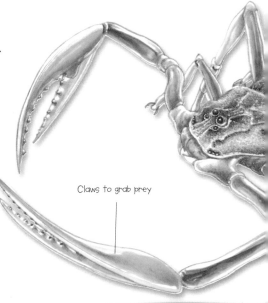

Claws to grab prey

449 The marine toad produces venom from special areas, called glands, behind its eyes. The venom is not used to kill prey, but to protect the toad from being eaten by other animals because it is extremely poisonous if swallowed.

450

Many snakes have venom glands in their mouths. They use their fangs to inject poison straight into their victim's body. Venom is made from saliva mixed with deadly substances. Spitting cobras shoot venom from their mouths. This venom can cause blindness in humans.

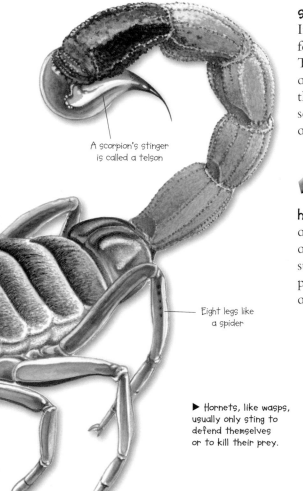

A scorpion's stinger is called a telson

Eight legs like a spider

▶ Hornets, like wasps, usually only sting to defend themselves or to kill their prey.

451

Scorpions belong to the same group as spiders – arachnids. Instead of producing venom in their fangs, they have stings in their tails. They use venom to kill prey, such as lizards and mice, or to defend themselves. Few scorpions can cause serious injury to humans, but some, such as the death stalker scorpion, are deadly.

452

Even small insects can harm other animals. Hornets, wasps and bees have stings in their tails that are attached to venom sacs. A single sting causes swelling and pain, and may prove fatal to people who are allergic to the venom.

Sting

Scary snakes

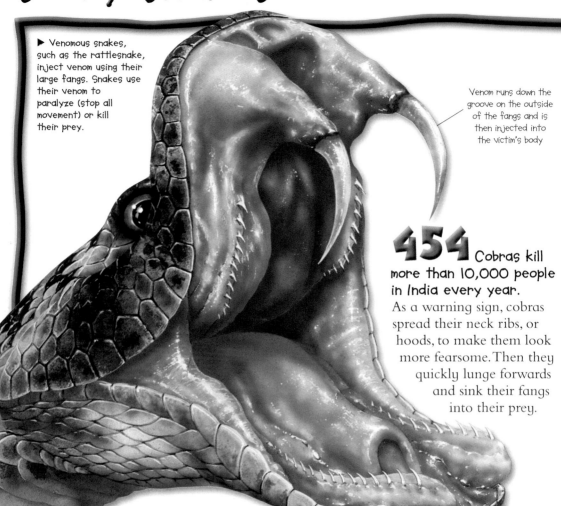

▶ Venomous snakes, such as the rattlesnake, inject venom using their large fangs. Snakes use their venom to paralyze (stop all movement) or kill their prey.

Venom runs down the groove on the outside of the fangs and is then injected into the victim's body

454 Cobras kill more than 10,000 people in India every year. As a warning sign, cobras spread their neck ribs, or hoods, to make them look more fearsome. Then they quickly lunge forwards and sink their fangs into their prey.

453 With unblinking eyes, sharp fangs and flickering tongues, snakes look like menacing killers. Despite their fearsome reputation, snakes only attack people when they feel threatened.

455 The taipan is one of Australia's most venomous snakes. When this snake attacks, it injects large amounts of venom that can kill a person in less than an hour.

456 Carpet vipers are small snakes found throughout many parts of Africa and Asia. They are responsible for hundreds, maybe thousands, of human deaths every year. Carpet viper venom affects the nervous system and the blood, causing the victim to bleed to death.

I DON'T BELIEVE IT!

Snakes can open their jaws so wide that they can swallow their prey whole. Large snakes, such as constrictors, can even swallow antelopes or pigs!

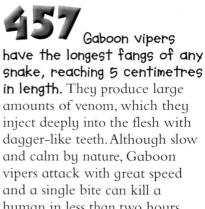

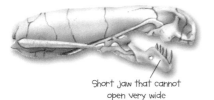

◀ Primitive snakes have a heavy skull with a short lower jaw and few teeth.

Short jaw that cannot open very wide

◀ Rear-fanged snakes have fangs in the roof of their mouths.

Fangs are towards the rear of the mouth, below the eye

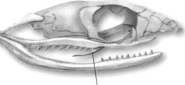

◀ Some snakes have fangs at the front of their mouths.

The fangs are hollow, and positioned at the front of the mouth

457 Gaboon vipers have the longest fangs of any snake, reaching 5 centimetres in length. They produce large amounts of venom, which they inject deeply into the flesh with dagger-like teeth. Although slow and calm by nature, Gaboon vipers attack with great speed and a single bite can kill a human in less than two hours.

▶ Snakes kill their prey with a lethal bite. Then they swallow the victim, such as a rodent, whole.

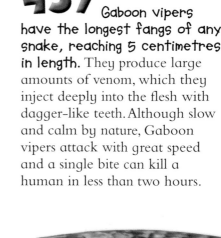

Dragons and monsters

▼ Komodo dragons use their powerful jaws to tear the flesh of their victim, and then eat everything, including bones and fur.

458 Komodo dragons are not really dragons, but lizards. They can reach 3 metres in length and up to 100 kilograms in weight, making them the largest lizards in the world. They hunt their prey using their sensitive sense of smell.

459 Once the Komodo has caught its prey, it sinks its sharp teeth into the victim's flesh. With a mouth full of poisonous bacteria, one bite is enough to kill an animal with an infection, even if it escapes the Komodo's clutches.

460 There are only two truly poisonous lizards — the Gila monster and the Mexican beaded lizard. Gila monsters live in North America and they have bands of black, pink and yellow on their scaly skin to warn predators to stay away.

▲ Gila monsters use their sense of smell to hunt small animals and find reptile eggs. They can kill their prey with a single bite.

▼ Fire salamanders are amphibians, like frogs. They hunt insects and earthworms, mainly at night.

461 Fire salamanders look like a cross between a lizard and a frog. They have bold patterns on their skin to warn predators that they are poisonous. The poison, or toxin, is on their skin and tastes foul. They squirt the toxin at predators, irritating or even killing them.

Fearsome frogs

462 At first glance, few frogs appear fearsome. They may not have teeth or claws, but frogs and toads produce a deadly substance in their moist skin. This substance may taste foul or even be poisonous. The most poisonous frogs live in the forests of Central and South America. They are called poison-dart frogs.

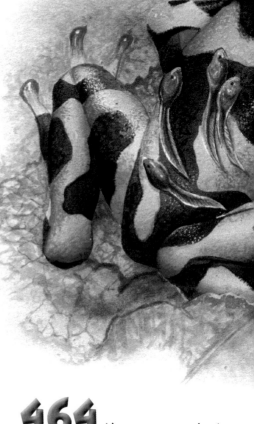

463 One of the deadliest frogs is the golden poison-dart frog. It lives in rainforests in western Colombia, and its skin produces a very powerful poison – one of the deadliest known substances. A single touch is enough to cause almost instant death.

▼ The strawberry poison-dart frog is also known as the 'blue jeans' frog because of its blue legs.

464 Many poison-dart frogs are becoming rare in the wild. This is because the rainforests where they live are being cut down. Some poison-dart frogs can be kept in captivity, where they gradually become less poisonous. When they are raised in captivity, these frogs are not poisonous at all.

◀ The male green poison-dart frog carries tadpoles on his back. He takes them to a safe place in water where they will grow into adults.

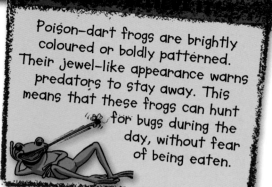

Poison-dart frogs are brightly coloured or boldly patterned. Their jewel-like appearance warns predators to stay away. This means that these frogs can hunt for bugs during the day, without fear of being eaten.

465 People who live in the rainforests of Central and South America use the poison from frogs to catch food. A hunter wipes the tip of a dart on the poisonous frog's back, then carefully puts it in a blowpipe. One puff sends the lethal dart into the body of an unsuspecting monkey or bird.

▼ Poison is wiped off the back of the golden poison-dart frog with a dart. One frog produces enough poison for more than 50 darts.

466 Looking after eggs is the job of male green poison-dart frogs. The female lays her eggs amongst the leaf litter on the forest floor. The male guards them until they hatch into tadpoles, then carries them to water, where they will grow into frogs.

Eight-legged hunters

467 Many people believe that the deadliest spider is the tarantula. These hairy spiders may look like monsters, but they don't really deserve their killer reputation. Tarantulas rarely bite humans, and not all tarantulas are venomous.

▲ After an insect becomes trapped in the spider's web, the spider kills it with a venomous bite. The spider will eat almost every part of its prey.

469 Tarantulas hunt their prey, such as insects, frogs and lizards, rather than spinning webs. They use their large fangs to inject venom into their prey and crush it into a pulp. Digestive juices are poured over the victim until it turns into a liquid and can be sucked up.

468 Black widow spiders are one of the most dangerous spiders in the world, but they only attack if disturbed. A bite from a male is nothing to worry about, but a bite from a female may prove fatal.

◄ Female black widow spiders use their poison not only to catch prey, but also to kill their partners after mating.

470 Spiders belong to a group of animals called arachnids, along with scorpions and ticks. Some ticks can kill without using deadly poison. They attach themselves to the bodies of humans and other animals, and suck their blood. This can spread deadly diseases.

QUIZ

1. How do ticks kill animals?
2. Is the male or female black widow spider more dangerous?
3. Which spider stands on its hind legs when it feels threatened?

Answers:
1. They suck their blood and spread diseases 2. Female 3. Funnel web spider

471 There are many types of funnel web spider, and some of them are very venomous. When a funnel web spider is threatened, it stands on its hind legs and rears, showing its huge fangs. These killers bite their prey many times, injecting poison.

▲ The fangs of the funnel web spider are so strong that they can pierce human skin, even fingernails. Its bite can cause death in just 15 minutes.

Clever defenders

472 To survive in a dangerous world, animals need to be able to hide, fight, or appear deadly. When it is threatened, the spiny puffer fish swallows large amounts of water, making its body swell up and its spines stand on end.

473 Spines can be used to pass venom into the victim's body, or used as weapons of defence. The long, sharp spines on the Cape porcupine are called quills, and they stick into an attacker's body, causing painful injuries.

▼▶ The spiny puffer fish stiffens and swells its body, changing from an ordinary-looking fish to a spiky ball.

◄ Tortoises are protected from predators by their tough shell. Even the sharp claws and teeth of lion cubs cannot break it.

474
Some animals hide from their predators using camouflage. This means the colour or pattern of an animal's skin blends in with its surroundings. Lizards called chameleons are masters of camouflage. They can change their skin colour from brown to green so they blend in with their background. They do this to communicate with one another.

475
The bold colours and pattern on the coral snake's skin warns predators that it is poisonous. The milk snake looks almost identical to the coral snake, but it is not venomous. Its colour keeps it safe though, because predators think it is poisonous.

I DON'T BELIEVE IT!

Electric eels have an unusual way of staying safe — they zap prey and predators with electricity! They can produce 600 volts of power at a time, which is enough to kill a human!

▶ The harmless milk snake looks similar to the venomous coral snake, so predators stay away. This life-saving animal trick is called mimicry.

Danger at sea

476 Deep in the ocean lurk some of the deadliest creatures in the world. There are keen-eyed killers, venomous stingers and sharp-toothed hunters, but as few of these animals come into contact with humans, attacks are rare.

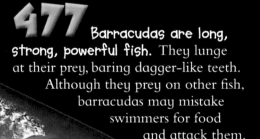

▶ The Australian box jellyfish is also known as the sea wasp. Its tentacles can grow more than 3 metres in length and one animal has enough venom to kill 60 people.

477 Barracudas are long, strong, powerful fish. They lunge at their prey, baring dagger-like teeth. Although they prey on other fish, barracudas may mistake swimmers for food and attack them.

478 The box jellyfish is one of the most lethal creatures in the world. A touch from only one tentacle can kill a human. The floating body of a jellyfish is harmless, but danger lies in the many tentacles that drift below. Each tentacle is covered with tiny stingers that shoot venom into the victim.

◀ Barracudas are fierce fish with powerful jaws and sharp teeth.

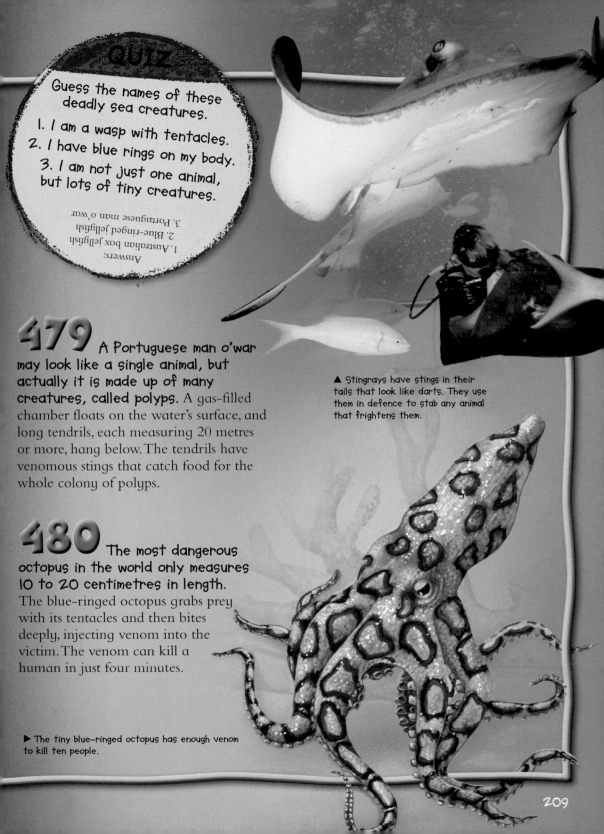

479 A Portuguese man o'war may look like a single animal, but actually it is made up of many creatures, called polyps. A gas-filled chamber floats on the water's surface, and long tendrils, each measuring 20 metres or more, hang below. The tendrils have venomous stings that catch food for the whole colony of polyps.

▲ Stingrays have stings in their tails that look like darts. They use them in defence to stab any animal that frightens them.

480 The most dangerous octopus in the world only measures 10 to 20 centimetres in length. The blue-ringed octopus grabs prey with its tentacles and then bites deeply, injecting venom into the victim. The venom can kill a human in just four minutes.

▶ The tiny blue-ringed octopus has enough venom to kill ten people.

Sharks in the shadows

481 Few animals send a shiver down the spine quite like a great white shark. This huge fish is a skilled hunter. Its bullet-shaped body can slice through the water at lightning speed, powered by huge muscles and a crescent-shaped tail.

482 Sharks are fish, and belong to the same family as rays and skates. Most sharks are predators and feed on fish, squid, seals and other sea creatures. Some sharks hunt with quick spurts of energy as they chase their prey. Others lie in wait for victims to pass by.

483 One of the deadliest sharks can be found in oceans and seas throughout the world. Blue sharks often hunt in packs and circle their prey before attacking. Although these creatures normally eat fish and squid, they will attack humans.

484 Bull sharks are a deadly threat to humans. This is because they live in areas close to human homes. They often swim inland, using the same rivers that people use to bathe and collect water, and may attack.

▲ Great white sharks are fearsome predators. They have rows of ultra-sharp triangular teeth that are perfect for taking large bites out of prey, such as seals, sea lions and dolphins.

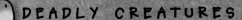

485 Grey reef sharks are sleek, swift predators of the Indian and Pacific oceans. Unusually, they give plenty of warning before they attack. If the grey reef shark feels threatened, it drops its fins down, raises its snout and starts weaving and rolling through the water.

Peril at the shore

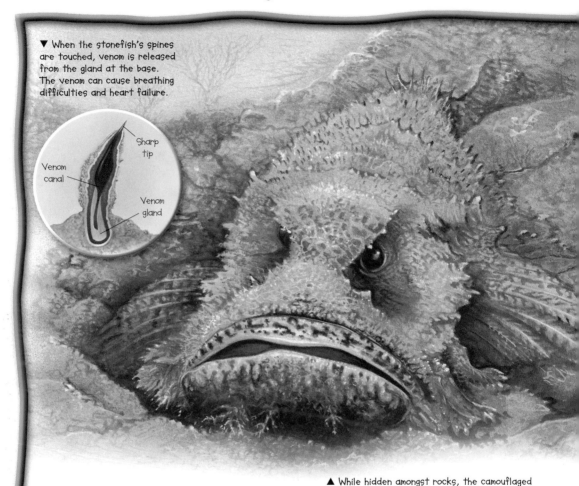

▼ When the stonefish's spines are touched, venom is released from the gland at the base. The venom can cause breathing difficulties and heart failure.

Sharp tip

Venom canal

Venom gland

▲ While hidden amongst rocks, the camouflaged stonefish waits for its prey, such as small fish.

486 The seashore may seem like a quiet place, but danger lies beneath the gently lapping waves. While some predators actively hunt their prey, some creatures just sit and wait.

487 Stonefish may look like a piece of rocky coral, but their cunning disguise hides a deadly surprise. One touch of the sharp spines on the stonefish's back results in an injection of venom, which may be fatal.

DESIGN TIME

You've now read about lots of dangerous animals and the tools they use to kill their prey. Now it's time to draw or paint your own deadly creature.

Will it have claws, fangs, spikes, venom or horns? What will you call it? Perhaps a clawfish or a dragon monkey?

489 Sea snakes spend their lives in water. They breathe air, so they need to keep returning to the surface. All sea snakes are poisonous, and although their bites are painless at first, the venom is very powerful and can kill.

490 Seashells are not always as harmless as they appear. Rather than chasing their prey, cone shells attack other animals using a poison that paralyzes the victim so it cannot escape. The venom of fish-eating cone shells can paralyze a fish within seconds. Although their venom can be fatal to humans, it is being used by scientists to develop medicines that reduce pain.

488 Lionfish are graceful swimmers, but the long spines on their fins inject venom as swiftly as a needle. A single injury from one spine causes immediate sickness and great pain, but it is unlikely to prove deadly to a human.

▼ Cone shells use their long proboscis to shoot a poisonous dart into their prey. The venom is very powerful and quickly paralyzes the prey.

213

Minibeasts

◀ Although houseflies do not have stings, they are dangerous to humans. They can spread diseases if they land on food.

491 **Animals don't have to be big to be beastly.** There are many small animals, particularly insects, that are killers. Some of them, such as ants, are predators that hunt to eat. Others, such as locusts, cause destruction that affects humans.

492 **Ants are found almost everywhere, except in water.** Most ants are harmless to humans, but army ants and driver ants turn tropical forests and woodlands into battlefields. The stings of army ants contain chemicals that dissolve flesh. Once their prey has turned to liquid, the ants can begin to drink it.

▼ Millions of army ants live in a single group, or colony. They hunt together, swarming through leaf litter and attacking anything in their way.

493 Driver ants have large jaws that can slice easily through food. They hunt in large numbers and swarm through forests hunting for prey. Driver ants can kill large animals, such as cows, by biting them to death. They have also been known to strip a chicken down to its skeleton in less than a day.

▲ Killer bees fiercely protect their hive by swarming around it. They will attack anything that approaches the nest.

494 Deadly plagues of locusts have been written about for thousands of years. When they search for food, they travel in swarms of millions, eating all the plants they encounter. This can leave humans without any food.

495 Killer bees are a new type of bee that was created by a scientist. He was hoping to breed bees that made lots of honey, but the bees proved to be extremely aggressive. Killer bees swarm in huge groups and when one bee stings, the others quickly join in. One sting is not deadly, but lots of bee stings can kill a human. It is thought that about 1000 people have been killed by these minibeasts.

The enemy within

496 Many deadly creatures are too small to be seen. They are parasites, living on or inside the body of humans or animals, causing harm, disease and even death. An animal that is home to a parasite is called a host.

▼ The Black Death, or bubonic plague, was spread by rats and it wiped out one-third of Europe's population (25 million people) about 700 years ago.

497 Rats are known to spread disease. They carry bacteria on their paws and in their mouths, but they also carry another type of parasite called fleas. Even the fleas can have parasites inside their bodies – plague bacteria.

498 Humans have suffered from plagues for thousands of years. These diseases are spread when rat fleas bite people, spreading the plague bacteria. Plague usually only occurs when people live in dirty conditions where rats and their fleas can breed. Plague can spread quickly, wiping out millions of lives.

▼ Tsetse flies feed on blood and spread parasites that cause sleeping sickness. This painful disease is common in developing countries and leads to death if not treated.

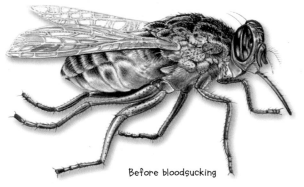

Before bloodsucking

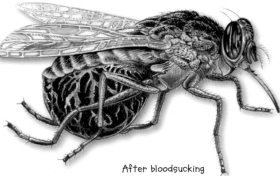

After bloodsucking

QUIZ

1. Which plague wiped out about one-third of Europe's population?
2. How do mosquitoes spread malaria and other diseases?
3. Which parasites do rats carry?

Answers:
1. The Black Death
2. By sucking the blood of their victims 3. Fleas

499 Some of the most common parasites are worms. Tiny threadlike worms called nematodes live inside the bodies of most animals, including some humans. Nematodes can spread disease. Tapeworms belong to a different family of worms called flatworms. They absorb food from their host's intestine.

▶ Mosquitoes pierce the skin of the victim to suck their blood, spreading deadly diseases, such as malaria.

500 The mosquito and its tiny parasites are among the deadliest creatures in the world. When mosquitoes suck human and animal blood, they pass parasites into the host's body, including the parasite that causes malaria. Malaria is a disease that mainly affects people living in hot countries in the developing world. It causes about one million deaths a year in Africa.

Index

Page numbers in **bold** indicate main entries; page numbers in *italics* indicate illustrations.

Index

Index

Acknowledgements

The publishers would like to thank the following sources for the use of their photographs:

t = top, h = bottom, l = left, r = right

Page 87 New Line/Everett/Rex features; 104 Shawn P. Carey (Migration Productions); 105 Laurie Goodrich, Hawk Mountain Sanctuary, USA; 129(b) David Norton/rspb-images.com

Alamy 106–107 A & J Visage; 117 blickwinkel; 129(t) Peter Arnold, Inc.

Ardea.com 133(t) M. Watson; 143 Francois Gohier/Ardea London Ltd; 145(cr) John Cancalosi; 154 Chris Harvey

Corbis 43(tr) William Dow; 52 Renee Lynn; 59(t) Frank Leonhardt/dpa; 74–75 CLARO CORTES IV/Reuters; 79 Kevin Schafer; 80 Kennan Ward; 89 Steve Klaver/Star Ledger; 110(bl) Arthur Morris; 120–121 W. Perry Conway; 125 Sandor H.Szabo/epa; 130 Ralph Clevenger; 156 David A. Northcott

Dreamstime.com 145(tr) Picstudio; 151(top inset) Sharkegg

FLPA 19(bl) Frans Lanting/Minden Pictures; 29(tr) Gerard Lacz; 42(b) Rob Reijnen/Foto Natura; 47(tr) Frans Lanting/Minden Pictures; 49(b) Martin B Withers; 54 Michio Hoshino/Minden Pictures; 55 Derek Middleton; 60 L Lee Rue; 64 JIM BRANDENBURG/Minden Pictures; 69 FLIP NICKLIN/Minden Pictures; 70 Mike Lane; 72(t) SUMIO HARADA/Minden Pictures,(b) Frans Lanting; 75(t) Terry Whittaker; 77 Michael Gore; 88 Yva Momatiuk/John Eastcott/Minden Pictures; 90 Jim Brandenburg/Minden Pictures; 91 Gerry Ellis/Minden Pictures; 115 Imagebroker, Bernd Zoller, Image; 119 Ramon Navarro/Minden Pictures; 123 Roger Tidman; 131(t) Frans Lanting; 133(b) Mark Newman; 138(tr) Norbert Wu/Minden Pictures; 139(tr) Michael & Patricia Fogden/Minden Pictures; 144(l) Michael & Patricia Fogden/Minden Pictures; 166 Colin Marshall; 170–171 Michael & Patricia Fogden/Minden Pictures; 203 Mark Moffett/Minden Pictures; 208(t) Panda Photo

Fotolia.com 108 javarman; 136(panel, clockwise from top right)Becky Stares, Vatikaki, Eric Gevaert, reb; 138(b) Paul Murphy; 181 Carlton Mceachern; 191 Eric Gevaert; 199 Ami Beyer; 204 Reiner Weidemann

Getty 158–159 Digital Vision; 167(b) Marc Crumpler

iStockphoto.com 141(t) Ameng Wu; 144(tr) Mark Kostich; 146(bl) Seth Ames; 148(tl) lara seregni; 151(b) Mark Kostich; 157(cr) Mark Kostich; 162(br) Eric Isselée; 164(bl) Dave Rodriguez; 167(t) Claude Robidoux; 174(t) Roman Lipovskiy

NHPA 162(tl) Daniel Heuclin; 174(b) Tony Crocetta; 201 Daniel Heuclin; 215 Martin Harvey

naturepl.com 92–93 Wild Wonders of Europe/Nill; 96(t) Igor Shpilenok; 97(t) Tony Heald, (br) John Cancalosi; 101 Markus Varesvuo; 102 Juan Carlos Munoz; 110–111 Markus Varesvuo; 113 Luis Quinta; 132 John Cancalosi; 140(b) Daniel Gomez; 149(b) Tim MacMillan/John Downer Pr; 175(t) John Cancalosi; 189 Bruce Davidson

photolibrary.com 66–67; 73; 82; 134–135 Berndt Fischer; 137(b) Werner Bollmann; 139(b) David B Fleetham; 145(b) Zigmund Leszczynski; 146–147 Jack Goldfarb; 152–153 John Cancalosi; 153 Carol Farneti Foster; 169(tr) Morales Morales; 175(b) Imagesource; 216

Photoshot 96(br) Andy Rouse; 109 Jordi Bas Casas; 116 Jordi Bas Casas

All other photographs are from: Corel, digitalSTOCK, digitalvision, Fotolia.com, ImageState, iStockphoto.com, John Foxx, PhotoAlto, PhotoDisc, PhotoEssentials, PhotoPro, Stockbyte

Every effort has been made to acknowledge the source and copyright holder of each picture. Miles Kelly Publishing apologises for any unintentional errors or omissions.

All artworks from the Miles Kelly Artwork Bank